Wisconsin
Blue-Ribbon Trout Streams

By R. Chris Halla

Wisconsin
BLUE-RIBBON
Trout Streams

R. Chris Halla

Frank Amato

PORTLAND

Dedication

This book is for Janet, the best fishing partner a fellow could hope for.

Acknowledgments

Herein, you will encounter, in words and pictures and spirit,
my fishing "buddies;" the people I fish with; the people I wish I could fish with
(or could have fished with) more often; teachers and students; friends and relatives; strange cats and stray cats. They are—in no particular order, because you never know who can go fishing when: My son Josh and his wife Lisa; my granddaughter Nia; my brother Floyd, my nephews Denny and Craig; my nephew Erik; my brothers-in-law Kirk and Brian; Tom and Kathy Magnuson; Gary Busha; Mary Radtke; Dan Wendelborn; John Judson; Mike Monson; Chuck Richards; Troy Wise; Dad and Mom and Rachel; and all those other friends and good strangers who shared stories, notes, flies, beers and streamtime.

Special thanks to Amy Vanden Oever for her ongoing encouragement and for her help with this project.
Some of the river profiles presented here have appeared in somewhat different or abbreviated form in *Midwest Fly Fishing.*
Thanks are extended to Editor & Publisher Tom Helgeson for giving the Middle a place to speak in its own voice.
Thanks to Rich Osthoff and Bob White for developing some of my favorite fly patterns, sharing them and thereby putting me into fish when others could only watch and wonder. Thanks to bug meister, Dean Hansen, of Stillwater, Minnesota for sharing just a fraction of his knowledge and some of his fantastic photographs.
Thanks to Matt and Laurie Supinski and Rich Brown for sharing their "big fish" photos.
Thanks to Janet, as well as Tom Montag, Don Heemstra, Josh Halla, Denny Halla and Troy Wise for wielding the camera so that I could be in a few of the pictures.

Frank Amato Publications, Inc.
P.O. Box 82112, Portland, Oregon 97282
503•653•8108 • www.amatobooks.com

All Photographs by Chris Halla unless otherwise noted.
All photography © R. Chris Halla; Cover photo © R. Chris Halla
Fly Plates © Jim Schollmeyer
Book and Cover Design: Kathy Johnson

Printed in Singapore

Softbound ISBN: 1-57188-161-1   UPC: 0-66066-00359-1

1 3 5 7 9 10 8 6 4 2

Contents

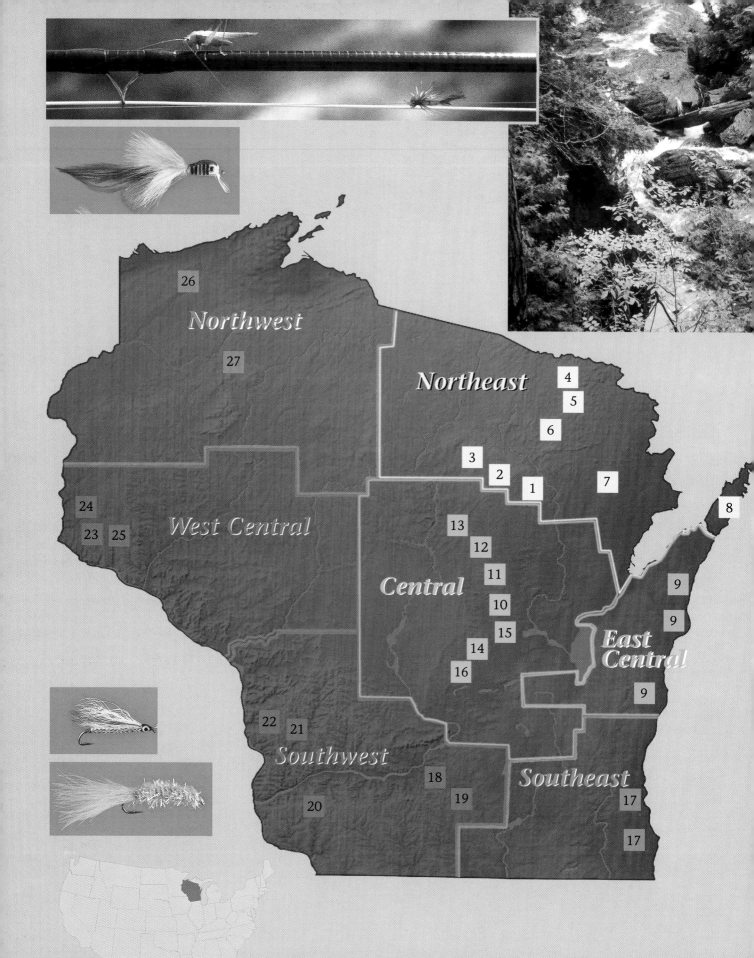

Northwest

Northeast

West Central

Central

East Central

Southwest

Southeast

The Rivers:

Fishing the Badger State

Sometimes, after parking near my favorite spot on my favorite trout stream, I climb over the stile on the west side of the skinny, gravel road and skulk down to the wide, slow water below the bridge.

Sometimes I go east and upstream.

Long casts onto the mixed black currents directly under the bridge are reserved for days when my ego needs a boost. The fish that live under the bridge are large. Thanks to low light and a few large rocks to stir the passing water, they are easy to catch...usually...well, if you know how.

The other way—east, upstream—takes more skill. The stream is narrow, zigzagging through open meadow. You have to stay low and quiet. You have to sneak. Often as not, you have to cast from your knees. Did I mention that the slightest visible movement, the slightest sound, to say nothing of a bad cast, will put the fish down for an hour or more, maybe for the rest of the day? These are brown trout: Their brains may be tiny, but their instincts are honed to razor's edge sharp.

If you manage to make a cast without spooking the fish that sit along the current seam, your fly must drop to the water in nearly flawless imitation of a real bug and drift, without a hint of drag, downstream. Your eyes follow as it bounces on the surface back toward you. You hold your breath, because you can't help it. A trout appears below your fly.

Sip....

A subtle rise punctuates the stream with a dimple where your fly had been. Your hand and arm pull back as your mind calculates the sum of what has just occurred. The trout shakes its head and pulls as though it has transformed itself, first into a dog with a pull toy, then into a submerged log...a log that swims...fast...in several directions...all at once. The sensation telegraphs from hook through tippet-leader-line-rod-hand to throbbing forearm.

You pull back a little harder to be sure the hook is set. The trout tries to run, turns to rocks and weeds, turns to underwater tree stump, but can neither find refuge nor break your line on any of it. Your rod is out and slightly up at 30 degrees, or a little less, because your arm remembers having learned that this angle will give you an advantage and shorten the fight.

You strip line until the fish is under control, then go to the reel. Now, more quickly than you'd expected, the fish is at hand. A 17-inch, wild brown trout gasps for air through gills while you pop the hook out and stall her, nose-to-current, until she can swim away and survive to be caught another day.

Every second that has just passed is typical of fishing Wisconsin's blue-ribbon trout streams.

10,000 Miles Of Diversity

In the Badger State there are nearly 10,000 miles of trout water divided among some 2,500 trout streams. There are big, famous, freestone rivers populated by browns and rainbows. There are limestone-bedded chalk streams, seldom wider than a village street. There are forest creeks, often as narrow as a sidewalk, full to bursting with brookies. And there are the "east coast" waters that flow into Lake Michigan, and run with steelhead and salmon throughout the year.

While there are many surprises to be found in Wisconsin trout fishing, there are some generalities to keep in mind. In the north, streams are more likely to flow through woods or forest; in the south, through meadow or pasture. (Although, exceptions are easy to find.) One stream may flow along the roadway, offering numerous pull-offs, while another may take a long hike from your parked vehicle to get to the best spots. Excellent fishing can be found right in the middle of some towns or cities, including Milwaukee, the state's largest city.

Brown trout may be found almost everywhere in Wisconsin. Brookies are most abundant in the northern half of the state, but there are also healthy populations elsewhere. New programs, practices and stream restorations have paid off with numerous, and larger, brook trout where they have been scarce for years. Rainbows exist here and there throughout the state, with limited natural reproduction.

In a 1999 Trout Unlimited study researched and written by University of Wisconsin biologist Stephanie Lindloff and TU's Conservation Geneticist John Epifanio, "Wisconsin leads the nation in stream miles designated as 'high quality' waters. The study credits the state's tradition of protecting and restoring habitat for naturally reproducing trout. The study also recognizes Wisconsin's Trout Stamp program as being "unique in dedicating virtually 100 percent of trout stamp funds to trout habitat acquisition and restoration."

If you were to fall out of the sky and land on Wisconsin, you would be very likely to touch down within walking distance of a trout stream. At worst, you would still be within an hour's drive. And, in addition to all that free-flowing, cold trout water, Wisconsin offers many more miles of rivers and streams, as well as 15,000 inland lakes, hundreds of miles of coast along the inland seas of Michigan and Superior, and numerous spring and farm ponds hosting over 150 cold- and warmwater species of fish. Besides the trout, panfish, walleye, smallmouth and largemouth bass, northern pike and the legendary muskie are waiting to test your skills.

Preferred Tackle

My own preference for almost all but steelhead and salmon (and northern pike and muskie) fishing is a three- to five-weight rod between 6 1/2 and 8 1/2 feet long, coupled to a gray, green or tan floating fly line, with a nine- to 12-foot leader, ending in a 5X, 6X or 7X tippet. I know there's the trend to smaller and finer, but a combination of super-light rod and ultrafine tippet is too hard on the fish. And, remember, that fight that gives us such pleasure is not near as much fun to the fish. Better to use tackle that allows you to fight and land fish fast so that they may be returned to the water with a better chance of survival.

For the biggest fish, step up to six- to nine-weight lines and rods of 8 1/2 to 10 feet in length, and leaders from 7 1/2 to 9-feet long. Whereas an inland stream trout, no matter how big, will seldom tear off line faster than you can keep up, some of the bruisers of the Lake Michigan and Lake Superior tributaries, as well as the pike and muskies that inhabit some of our rivers and flowages, will put you into your backing before you know what hit.

A Basic Fly Selection

More specific comment on the best flies for each stream (including a number of regional and local favorites) are detailed throughout this book. The notes that follow are simply a primer; something to get you started if you haven't fished here before. Not surprisingly, these are flies that have been found to be a good start point for almost anywhere in the country. Sometimes I think you could fish with nothing but these 15 flies and still never have a bad day as long as you knew which to use when.

Dry flies: #14-20 Adams; #14-20 Black Gnat; #16-22 Blue-Winged Olive; #12-18 Elk Hair Caddis; #10-16 Royal Wulff.
Nymphs: #10-16 Gold Ribbed Hare's Ear; #10-16 March Brown; #10-16 Pheasant Tail; #10-16 Prince; #10-16 Olive Scud.

Streamers: #6-12 Mickey Finn; #4-12 Little Brook Trout.
Terrestrials: #14-20 Black Ant; #8-14 Dave's Cricket; #6-12 Joe's Hopper.

To this base selection, add bead heads to the nymphs, beads and BBs to the streamers, and trim the hackles and wings on your dries in response to whatever is or isn't happening at the moment. Onstream modifications can account for a dramatic increase in hook-ups. As you travel from stream to stream, broaden your selection according to information you find here or there garnered from fellow fishers you meet in the course of your fishing day. Add to your box liberally with local favorites *and* local spins on classic patterns.

A little Door County stream empties into Lake Michigan.

Stream Bottoms, Cautions and Dangers

Folks have gotten used to grizzly, cat and rattler stories out of the West. Once you get left of the Mississippi, you accept the possibility of certain encounters: Encounters of the most unpleasant kind with mammals, snakes, nasty plants, bugs and the water itself. These are all part of the adventure. The good news—and the bad news—is that Wisconsin has its own set of adventure-enhancing experiences to offer, including variations on pretty much all of the above, with barbed wire and electric fences (and the rare, but occasional, gun-wielding private property enthusiast) thrown in for comic relief.

Water with Attitude: The biggest rivers make themselves rather obvious: If world-class kayakers are portaging a stretch of heavy water, you would probably have to be an idiot to try to wade that same stretch. If you look at the water, and the water looks back and says, "I will either kill you or make a mess of you in the trying," stay out of it. But there are also many pieces of big water that can be waded safely if approached with the proper caution. Don't wade any water without talking to other fishers and locals first to get a clear and immediate sense of what you might expect. Try not to enter any stretch of water as a total stranger. I don't want your family suing me because you couldn't take a little simple advice.

Wisconsin waters that offer the greatest surprise are those narrow, little streams with three- to four-foot undercuts, seven-foot deep bend pools and sucking muck that may not be quicksand, but can be equally life-affirming to someone who wasn't expecting it. This stuff has eaten many wading boots and scared the warts off more than one unsuspecting wader. Obviously, I can't tell you where every one of these dangerous little pieces of liquid geography are—I find a couple new ones every year myself—but I can advise caution. No matter where you fish, do ask others what to expect, and take care. Consider carrying a wading staff *everywhere*, not just where you *think* you'll need it.

As in all things, Wisconsin trout streams have a great variety of bottom types. Depending on where you fish, boulders, big rocks, cobble, gravel, sand, silt, the aforementioned muck, clay and layers of limestone make up the water's floor. In many parts of the Badger State you will encounter a mix of these stream-bottom types. All of them can cause you to trip, fall or in other ways come to harm. If I might repeat myself...take care.

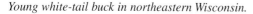

Young white-tail buck in northeastern Wisconsin.

Living, breathing dangers: Creatures and other life forms may not present the obvious threats in Wisconsin that they do elsewhere, but there are things you should be aware of. For simplicity's sake, I'll divide them by the following classifications: Mammals; snakes; bugs; and plants.

We do *not* have grizzly bears in Wisconsin. We also do *not* have cougars. (There are those nagging, occasional reports of

Wisconsin is home to a variety of snakes, but poisonous ones are few.

a black panther in western and central counties, but they've yet to prove out.) We *do* have rattlesnakes, but they appear to be extant only in the southwestern and west-central parts of the state (those areas edged by the Mississippi and St. Croix rivers). I personally have encountered them only in the extreme southwest, and then only on a couple of occasions, but my thinking is to err on the side of caution and accept that there are many who know more about such things than I do.

Mammals: Wisconsin has an impressive black bear population. The farther north you go, the more likely you are to be in proximity of them. Their range, however, does cover much of the state, and it appears to be expanding. Black bear have a whole different attitude than their grizzly cousins. Blacks typically take more of a "live and let live" attitude. It does, however, still make sense to take the usual precautions: Make plenty of noise, hang perishables out of reach, don't go to bed smelling like S'mores, and if you encounter a bear, give it the right of way. *Never* get between a sow and her cubs. If they do get upset, they're a lot bigger and tougher than you are. The happy fact is, as many black bear as we have here, your likelihood of running into one is limited.

Depending on where in Wisconsin you fish, you could also share space with wolves, bobcats or badgers (we're named after underground miners who were nicknamed after the flat-bodied, ill-tempered mammals, not the mammals themselves), but again, your chances of actually seeing one are quite rare. It should go without saying that if you *do* see one, you should respect the animal's space (he/she lives there, *you* do not) and observe standard precautions. The animals you are most likely to see, outside of the ever-present squirrels, rabbits, skunks, raccoons, opossums, woodchucks, beavers, muskrats, weasels and such, are coyote, foxes and white tail deer...especially white tail deer. (Keep this latter in mind when you're driving back to camp at night. Our roads are littered with white tails that didn't have a genetic imprint telling them that the sight of headlights does not mean "cross the road now.")

A special note on cows: If you fish Wisconsin trout streams, you will, at some time, be sharing your space with cows (and bulls). Those of you who have yet to be crowded into a barbed wire or electric fence, or a stream by a herd of nosy, young cows, or chased across a meadow by a bull that increases its speed and grows in size with every hoof beat, are as innocent and ignorant as a boy who has never given a cat a bath. Cows generally are as harmless as they are curious, but give them some room, stay out of the middle of a herd, and avoid fully equipped males completely.

Snakes: We have a nice variety of snakes in Wisconsin, but the emphasis would have to be on nice. To my knowledge, the only poisonous snake we have is the rattler. Otherwise, there are a number of big snakes (including bull snakes, fox snakes and pine snakes, which are often mistaken for rattlers), as well as garter, grass and other small snakes. As mentioned earlier, the known range of Wisconsin's rattlesnakes is quite limited.

Bugs: Our resident bugs range from annoying as hell to downright dangerous. The mosquitoes, of course, are legendary. (Some outdoorsmen insist the mosquito should be our designated state bird.) For most of us, a good dousing with bug dope (a steady diet of garlic doesn't hurt either) will keep the little bastards at bay. The insect vampires are more troublesome to some than others and severe reactions bear watching. We also have a number of spiders, the reactions to some of their bites less than amusing. The creeper most of us

Ephemerella needham.

need to be most cognizant of, because it is so common and so potentially dangerous, is the tick.

We have a variety of ticks in Wisconsin; all over Wisconsin. Wood ticks, bear ticks, deer ticks. In addition to all the other infections and discomforts these evil little bugs visit upon us, they (deer and bear ticks, in particular) are also the most common carriers and transmitters of Lyme disease. (Other insects, such as horseflies, deer flies *and* mosquitoes have been shown to carry the Lyme disease bacteria, and it is conceivable that these insects may also transmit Lyme disease.)

Your best defense against ticks (and other bugs) is to follow a standard procedure whenever you go afield (or astream).

1. Wear light-colored clothing. This will make ticks easier to see.
2. Tuck pants into boots or socks. Wear long sleeves, buttoned at the cuff. Waders may provide additional protection.
3. Apply tick/insect repellent to all clothing. Don't forget the outside of your vest and hat. Insect repellents that are safe for use directly on the skin should also be applied.
4. Walk in the center of mowed or beaten-down trails to minimize contact with vegetation.
5. Conduct thorough, full-body (and head) tick checks on yourself and your companions as soon as you get back to your vehicle or camp. This is no time to be bashful. (Depending on your feelings toward your companion or companions, however, it might be an opportunity to have a little extracurricular fun.)

If you find a tick on your person, remove it as soon as possible by grasping it with a tweezers and gently, but firmly pulling it straight out. If any part of the tick breaks off and remains imbedded, see a doctor. Wash the bite area and apply an antiseptic. Ticks, like grizzlies, big cats and rattlers, are not funny.

Plants: Poison ivy, poison oak, stinging nettle and a host of other plants known to cause everything from minor irritations to severe side effects are as common in Wisconsin as they are elsewhere. Waders help, of course, as do long sleeves. The simple, best advice is to be cautious, watch where you walk and where you put your hands. If you are especially sensitive to such things, come prepared: Assume that you *will* stumble or reach into the one plant that you are most sensitive to.

The Damned Weather: Count on this: While fishing in Wisconsin, you will encounter some form of extreme weather. It may be blistering heat, skull-numbing cold, torrential rains, drought, early spring or late fall blizzards, lightning, ferocious straight line winds or tornadoes. Years of sound advice from Mom and the TV weatherman should have taught you how to deal with these things using a common-sense approach. So why is it, that so many of us insist on standing in the middle of a river with our highly conductive graphite rods pointed to the sky as thunderstorms approach? Is it the dramatic back-lighting, in which we just look too damn good silhouetted against the rumbling, purple sky? The weather is serious business. When it turns ugly, head for cover.

The Regs & Categories

There are more than a few anglers who think Wisconsin's trout regs are way too complex and very confusing. The regs *are* complex, but between our *Wisconsin Trout Fishing Regulations and Guide* from the Wisconsin Department of Natural Resources (WDNR) and postings at many streams, they aren't—or at least they don't have to be—that confusing. The basics are very simple: The regular season runs from the first Saturday in May through September 30; As of this writing and into the foreseeable future, there is an early season on most inland streams that runs from March 1 to May 1 (artificial lures, barbless hooks and catch and release only); streams flowing into Lake Michigan may be fished all year upstream to the first dam or lake. Beyond that, there are details, special regs and subtleties that make having a current copy of the regulations handy at all times a necessity, but they really aren't difficult to deal with. (**Disclaimer: If you don't consult the current regs before you fish, don't blame me for the hassles you get yourself into.**)

Beyond the general trout-fishing regs, Wisconsin also has a category system geared to best managing each individual stream. While some stocking is practiced in many Wisconsin trout streams (and ponds and lakes), our focus is on natural reproduction, and the regs have as much to do with this as they

do with producing trophy trout. As long as you keep a copy of the *Trout Fishing Regulations and Guide* handy, as you travel, you shouldn't run into any problems.

There are five regulation categories.

Category 1: Minimum Size Limit: None; Daily Bag Limit: 10 (only 5 browns and rainbows).

Category 2: Minimum Size Limit: 7 inches; Daily Bag Limit: 5.

Category 3: Minimum Size Limit: 9 inches; Daily Bag Limit : 3.

Category 4: Minimum Size Limit: (brown and rainbow trout) 12 inches and (brook trout) 8 inches; Daily Bag Limit: 3.

Category 5: Special regulations; Size and Bag Limits vary by specific water and species. Special regs include everything from slot limits to Catch & Release only, and pretty much anything you could think of in-between.

A wild Wisconsin brook trout.

Again, there are subtleties. Consult the regs *before* you fish. If it all does sound too complex, remember, the Wisconsin regs are designed to create and maintain the healthiest possible resource management. And it *does* pay off...for the resource, and for all of us.

Stream Classification

In addition to the regulation's categories, Badger trout streams have been placed into three classes for fish management purposes. These classifications can be helpful in determining which rivers you wish to fish. For the latter reason, I've chosen to refer to them throughout this book. (As a general note of caution: Streams change, classifications change, and the information provided here is meant only as a guideline.)

The brown drake hatch brings up big browns on the Brule.

Wisconsin Blue-Ribbon Trout Streams

Challenging vegetation is part of the deal.

The descriptions that follow are (with minor editing and notations) as published originally by the WDNR.

Class 1: High-quality trout waters, having sufficient natural reproduction to sustain populations of wild trout at or near carrying capacity. Consequently, streams in this category require no stocking of hatchery trout. These streams or stream sections are often small and may contain small or slow-growing trout, especially in the headwaters. (They can also be large and contain monster trout.)

Class II: Streams in this classification may have some natural reproduction, but not enough to utilize available food and space. Therefore, stocking *sometimes* is required to maintain a desirable sport fishery. These streams show good survival and carryover of adult trout often producing some fish of better-than-average size.

Class III: Marginal trout habitat with little or no natural reproduction occurring. They require annual stocking of legal-size fish to provide trout fishing. Generally, there is little or no carryover of trout from one year to the next.

These classifications have been around for a long time, and as noted earlier, things do change; sometimes for the better. The good news is that, with Wisconsin's concentration on wild trout, some streams that were Class II or III are now Class I or II.

The Route We Will Follow

Think of the state as a clock (shaped like a mitten), its *north-east* corner falling in the area between midnight and somewhere around 2:30. We'll begin here and travel in a more or less clockwise direction, pausing after visiting the *east central* steelhead waters, to explore the trout-rich streams of *central* Wisconsin at our clock's center. From there we'll head to the *southeast*, then to the classic spring creeks of the *southwest* and on around to the hills and valleys of the *west central* region. We'll put a wrap on our Wisconsin tour in the *northwest* where Minnesota and Lake Superior define our edges.

Although I've chanced upon some wondrous water when my companions insisted I was lost and accused me of working with a broken map, you'll find that getting around is relatively easy, thanks to a number of map sources. For starters, the *Wisconsin Trout Fishing Regulations and Guide* includes color-coded maps showing the general location and regulation category for most Wisconsin trout waters. This, coupled with a DeLorme *Wisconsin Atlas & Gazetteer* may prove all many fishers need to maneuver from stream to stream. Wisconsin's Departments of Natural Resources, Tourism and Transportation all have maps and other visitor information available for the asking. There is, however, a great deal more available commercially as well. You will find a sampler of both commercial and non-commercial suppliers listed at the back of this book in the Sources & Resources section.

I hope you're able to stay with me...keep your way. If you can't, give me a call, and I'll try to help you get your bearings:

Where there are trout, there are great blue herons.

I'm in the book. (Be aware, however, that you may not find me home much during fishing season.)

Finding Your Way

You will *not* find, in this book, clear, concise, super-detailed directions to all of my or anyone else's favorite riffles, runs and pools. At the beginning of each chapter, you are given the region the stream is in, the county or counties it runs through and the nearest community or communities. Elsewhere in the text, you will encounter nearby or bordering roadways and occasional landmarks. If there is a fly or bait shop within relative proximity, it will be mentioned as well. Beyond that, it is up to you to employ a good set of maps and your own sense of adventure to find your own favorite riffles, runs, pools and the trout of your dreams.

Northeast

Wolf River

County: **Langlade**
Nearest Communities: **White Lake, Langlade, Pickerel, Shawano**
Fly/Bait Shop, Guide Service: **Mike's Mobile Service** (Langlade)**; Wolf River Fly Shop** (White Lake)

The Wolf River is born in Nicolet National Forest swampland that provides water to Hiles Mill pond, which drains into Pine Creek, which in turn feeds Pine Lake, which finally exits through three large culverts under Pine Lake Road as the Wolf River. People come to the headwaters of the Wolf from cities to the south to sit in row boats catching panfish on spin rods and cane poles, and at night to go to bed in red and yellow and blue cottages with signs out front that say things like "I'm-a-gun-a-get-away" and "All the Stroik's Goofer Gang." Signs that have meaning only to the people in the cottages. In winter they come here to ride their snowmobiles and to fish through holes in the ice.

A mile south of the lake and the cottages, the Wolf is beginning already to show signs of its unique character (although the trout don't come this far upstream).

This is North. The river-seamed swamp and forest country define the word "north." Going north by the compass or steering north by a star cannot help you comprehend North in the way this country can.

At Pearson, the Hunting River flows into the Wolf from the west. This is the point at which it is generally agreed the Wolf becomes a trout stream. The confluence of the Hunting and the Wolf is large, flat, just barely showing signs of movement. The Hunting can be a fairly good brook trout stream. A few of the colorful natives migrate into the Wolf to increase opportunities along this stretch when water temperatures are low. As the Wolf warms, the brookies head back to environs more forgiving of their delicate nature and their need for cold water. Access to both rivers is easy at this point.

The next easy access point downstream is where the County Highway A bridge crosses the river. At this point, the water picks up speed and becomes—as wading fishers and paddlers alike will tell you—more exciting, especially in spring and other times of high water. Just below the bridge is the first of many rapids between here and Menominee Tribal Lands where non-tribal fishing ends.

The Wolf at low flow in September.

Farther downstream, along Highway 55, is Military Park, a terrific place to picnic, a favorite put-in for paddlers and a pretty decent place to fish. The designer of this park must have been a fisher; there's no question he or she was a lover of rivers. This is a fine place to be standing in the water when the white flies (AKA *Ephoron leukon*; AKA White Wolfs—spelling of the latter by local preference) come off in August. A heavy white fly hatch, with the air full of them, is truly a sight to behold.

There is public access below Military Park at the village of Lily and at Big Sheen Rapids off Wolf Road (off Highway 55). Below these is Burnt Point Rapid, my favorite place on the Wolf. Hollister Road, an unpaved road that can be affected by heavy rains, takes you right up to the river. This too, is a pretty place to picnic, or have a beer, but the greatest attraction is, of course, the river. This part of the Wolf doesn't hold more fish than any other area—maybe fewer—but, as rivers go, it is aesthetically perfect. It took me aback the first time I saw it, and even now I am often struck speechless by its beauty. When I imagine the Wolf River, Burnt Point Rapid is the place my mind's eye sees. Here "boulder-strewn, freestone stream" is dramatically defined. This is a place to sit and watch a river for awhile. Unfortunately, the fishing is better both up- and downstream of Burnt Point.

Downstream from Burnt Point is the most popular stretch of the river for both fishers and floaters. There are places and times where the river craft virtually take over, and the fisher must wait his or her turn. "The aluminum hatch," Steve Nevala calls it. At times, however, when the aluminum hatch isn't *too* heavy, fishers and paddlers can coexist quite nicely. (This is not an experience confined to the Wolf in Wisconsin. It also occurs on a few of our other most canoeable waters; in particular the Peshtigo and Bois Brule, where fishers often become paddlers of necessity.)

Below Burnt Point, Nine-Mile Creek enters the Wolf, upriver a bit from the Soo Line Bridge where the big river's catch and release, artificials only section begins. On an unseasonably cold day in mid-September, my wife and I caught a pair of wild browns in Nine-Mile when the Wolf would surrender nothing. This was a switch from fishing feeders when the days are too warm.

At Langlade a sign announces:

Home of Gentle Ben
Raised and trained by Ivan Walters.

A historical marker tells the story of Langlade's beginnings. "The village of Langlade and Langlade County, were named for Charles Michel de Langlade, who has been called *The Father of Wisconsin*. Born at the trading post of Mackinac in 1729, de Langlade's character, military ability and influence left a commanding impression on Wisconsin's early history. He was among the first permanent settlers to locate on the present site of Green Bay about 1745. During the French and Indian War, de Langlade led Wisconsin Indians against Fort Duquesne

and from there to Fort Cumberland, where Braddock was in command, and where George Washington served as a young lieutenant. In 1759, de Langlade fought under General Montcalm in the Battle of Quebec, which ended the French Empire in North America. After active service with the British in the Revolutionary War, de Langlade returned to Green Bay. He died there in 1800."

Necessaries and Lodging
A fisher's immediate needs, with some limitations, can pretty much all be taken care of at Mike's Mobile Service in Langlade. And Bob Talasek's Wolf River Fly Shop would have to be considered a required stop for fly-fishers. Both are just off Highway 55.

Further south, at river's edge, is Buettner's Wild Wolf Inn where Herb Buettner is becoming a legend in his own time among fishers, floaters and river lovers in general. Although well-known already as a knowledgeable on-river resource, Buettner has made new friends for his efforts to restore wild rainbows to the Wolf (with the cooperation of the Menominees) and as one of many voices raised in the Crandon Mine controversy. (The latter posing a potentially serious on-going threat to the health of the Wolf and its tributaries.) Not far down from Buettner's, Menominee Tribal Lands (Menominee County) begin. Trout water extends about 25 miles into Menominee County, but by the time the river leaves the county, it has become a warmwater fishery known for its walleye fishing.

What to Fish With
There are about 35 miles of trout water on the Wolf above Menominee County. Browns, rainbows and occasional brookies populate the mostly Class II stream. There are a couple of dependable (some might even say legendary) hatches on the Wolf and others that can offer very good fishing, weather permitting.

Hendricksons, March browns and sulphurs all begin coming off in mid-May. The sulphurs are considered by some to be a super hatch. The fly most favored by local anglers when the sulphurs emerge is a #14-16 Sulphur tied with a light gray wing and a body of mixed yellow and orange. The sulphur hatch may last into mid-June, while the Hendricksons and March browns can both still be seen up to the end of June.

Brown drakes, yellow drakes and mahogany duns all appear in June and can stick around into July. Then in August, the Hexes and white flies make their appearances in what almost everyone agrees are true super hatches.

The Hex is not the giant *Hexagenia Limbata*, but a smaller mayfly often misidentified on the Wolf as a green drake. Hook size for this Hex would be #6-8, and more often the smaller of those.

The white fly, mentioned earlier, is best imitated by a #12 cream winged and bodied bug (White Wolf) or a sparsely dressed traditional White Wulff. Of all the many hatches on the Wolf, this is the most spectacular, as well as one of the most dependable.

This rainbow fell for a Brown Woolly bugger.

How To Fish

The first rule of fishing the Wolf is to keep moving. There are a lot of fish here, but there's also a lot of water, with the river averaging 50 yards and more in width. That means there isn't going to be a trout hiding in every perfect hiding place. You will have to put on some miles searching them out.

The second rule of fishing the Wolf is be careful; very careful. The Wolf is one of the most popular canoeing and kayaking rivers in Wisconsin by virtue of its steady flow and challenging rapids. Some of those white-water sections even the kayakers portage around. During periods of high water, early spring, in particular, is when the fastest water is at its most treacherous, but care is *always* advised. Wear proper wading boots, carry a staff and know when to stay out of the water.

Fish the pockets, the edges and pools below rapids. Especially when water temperatures rise in summer, many of the biggest fish will hide in the deepest pools and need to be dredged for with big, fast-sinking flies. One method that often proves effective on the Wolf is to quarter streamers and nymphs across then fish all the way through the drift and allow the fly to make a full swing before you begin your retrieve.

It may take a while to learn how to fish the Wolf effectively, but in the process you get a close-up look at one of the prettiest rivers and some of the most unspoiled country in Wisconsin.

Finding Your Way

Pick your way upstream along Highway 55, taking any of the westerly-heading roads that will put you at riverside pull-offs. Following County A west to County T will track you along the upper reaches of the Wolf's trout waters and to the mouth of the Hunting.

The best single resource available for newcomers to the Wolf is *Fly Fishing the Wolf River*, a 90-minute audio tape program (which includes a map, hatch chart and fly pattern guide). The program is part of the "River Rap Series" from Greycliff Publishing Company (P.O. Box 1273, Helena, MT 59624; 800/874-4171).

In addition to the mayflies, there are eastern salmon flies (#2-4) that appear between mid-May and mid-June, golden stones (#6-8) from mid-June to mid-July and little yellow sallies (#14-16) from mid-July through August. One day, after picnicking at Military Park, my friend Tom Montag stood at water's edge and watched while I threw large nymphs at holes behind boulders. Suddenly, or so it seemed, the air was full of huge bugs. I turned to point them out to Tom and saw that, unbeknownst to him, his legs were literally crawling with huge eastern salmon flies. Tom, being neither fisher nor giant bug fancier, found the experience disconcerting. Unfortunately, switching to an adult salmon fly pattern didn't help me catch any fish that day.

Finally, expect to find a variety of caddisflies on the Wolf throughout the season. Both varieties of blue-winged olives also appear for the better part of the season, as they do on most Wisconsin streams. For searching patterns, stick with a selection of the usual. For nymphs, Hare's Ears and Pheasant Tails are both good bets. Muddlers in tan and/or green, Black Nosed Dace, Little Brook Trout and Mickey Finns are all successful streamers. For dries, the two most popular searchers were both developed locally. The first, Cap's Hairwing (Hair Wing Adams in #10-16) was developed and made famous by Cap Buettner, Herb's brother and a true Wolf River legend himself. Second is the Close Carpet Fly, developed by George Close, who discovered that by adding Antron carpet fibers to a basic Compara Dun, he had a wildly effective trout attractant. The Close Carpet Fly is tied in sizes #8-12.

Northeast

East Branch
Eau Claire River

County: **Langlade**
Nearest Community: **Antigo**
Fly/Bait Shop, Guide Service: **Mike's Mobile Service** (Langlade); **Wolf River Fly Shop** (White Lake)

Even though I first fished the East Branch of the Eau Claire only a couple of years ago, there are things I've seen and experienced there that make it one of my favorite streams. On my first visit, it seemed to take forever to get my bearings and finally find an access point where someone else wasn't already parked. A quick scouting walk to the bridge from the car revealed a terrific-looking stretch of water, but no visible fish activity. In the time it took to go back to the car, assemble a rod and return to the bridge, a blue-winged olive hatch had started to come off that was quickly turning into a veritable cloud of airborne bugs. Trout were rising here and there, then everywhere. I almost fell on the rocks on my scramble down to the stream. Once in the water, my hands were shaking so badly I could barely tie on the #18 BWO Duck Shoulder Dun that matched the bugs in the air. I had never seen a hatch this thick and, so far, still haven't seen another. When the fishing began, it was a glorious half hour, maybe 40 minutes, of landing one small brook trout after another. The largest of them couldn't have been over nine inches, but there were so many...the water looked like it was boiling.

Later that same year, I headed upstream, on what had already become a favorite stretch of water, while my partners went downstream. I began catching fish immediately, first on a Brown Bivisible, then on an Adams: Not a day for exact imitations of anything. All the fish were of pretty good size for brookies; 10 to 13 honest inches. As I ducked to get under a low-hanging branch, I caught sight of a small whitetail doe crossing the stream at the next bend. When I reached that

A small specimen of
warmwater-tolerant Eau Claire brook trout.

bend, I heard her splash in the water around the next. And *there*, as I stood casting hopefully into a shallow riffle, I was startled by a noise at my side. It was the doe, within a few feet of me, looking me in the eye, showing no sign of fear. It seemed very strange until I saw the fawn standing behind her.

And last year...well, last year. In three trips to the East Branch, both my partners and I did well. But on our last visit, we saw something—yes, *we;* there *is* a second witness—that we could never have imagined had we not seen it. What we saw was brook trout. Two brook trout, and possibly a third. Very large brook trout. Their autumn colors made identification easy and immediate. First we saw them rise, almost simultaneously, with great commotion, at the top and bottom of the outside bend. And a few minutes later, we saw them swimming in a shallow pool. They were so big that I can't tell

Fungus as art on the river.

you how big, because you wouldn't believe me. Shortly thereafter, casting to the center of a deep alley where, again, there had been a huge rise, I had a hit and, thinking it to be Moby Trout or his sister, jerked back so hard with my rod that I nearly tore the head off a nine-inch brown with my fly in its jaw. This is why I am going back in spring with a box of meat-like flies and equipment twice as heavy as I often use here.

Vital Statistics

The East Branch offers up 11 miles of Class II trout water and another six of Class III. The brookies are wild natives with a unique (for brookies) ability to withstand, even thrive, when water temperatures climb as high as the low 80s on the warmest summer days. Another thing that makes the brook trout here unique is that they regularly grow to over 12 inches and into the teens. In our experience, nine to 12-inch fish are common, although there are still plenty of five-inch fish in the river too. Browns are planted in the East Branch, but, considering the potential for a race of super brookies, one has to wonder why.

The most productive trout waters are north and west of Antigo, above Highway 64, below County C and west of 45/47. Within that area, there are close to a dozen places to pull off with easy access. There are also trout to be found outside these boundaries, only in lower numbers. No, I am not going to tell you my favorite spot; I've already told you too much.

What To Fish With

In addition to the blue-winged olives, another standard you can count on throughout the season is an Elk Hair Caddis. I've tried a number of caddis patterns with success, but none have performed as consistently as a plain old Elk (or Deer) Hair. No matter what you fish with, if it doesn't draw a strike, try trimming the hackle off the bottom before you give up on it. Also expect Hendricksons the earliest part of the season, Sulphurs from mid-May to the end of June, light Cahills in June and July, and Tricos from mid-July to the end of the season. Look for Hexes beginning the middle of June and white flies in August. These latter two can, in a good year, provide phenomenal fishing, or so we're told.

We are told, too, that little yellow sallies can nicely represent the stonefly family during the summer months, but we have not experienced this personally. We've had some success with hoppers, crickets and ants as summer wears on; especially a #10 black and brown Dave's Cricket. If you like streamer fishing, try a standard Muddler, a brown and olive Woolly Bugger or a Little Brook Trout down-and-across with a full swing at the bottom. And, of course, for early morning and evening, well into dark, there are the meat flies; mice, frogs, big crayfish, hummingbirds, what-have-you.

Food, Lodging, Etceteras

Considering the close proximity of Antigo, food, lodging, supply and entertainment needs are easily met. Antigo is not a big town, but it has everything you are likely to need, as well as some of those things that, while not an absolute necessity, are nice to have (like live music with a little space to dance in). Lodging varies from the standard list of chain and mom and pop motels, to B&Bs and campgrounds. There is also a very sufficient selection of cafes, restaurants, supper clubs and taverns to meet your dining needs and desires. (This may be northern Wisconsin, but there *are* places that serve food that isn't deep fried or drowned in cheese.) The two food stops I would plan to make on any visit would be Gunkel's Bakery, for morning fare, and Blackjack Steakhouse, for dinner; the latter a nice combination of traditional American steakhouse and Wisconsin supper club.

Two-net Mary Radtke lands her first wild trout on a fly.

Prairie River

Counties: **Lincoln, Langlade**
Nearest Communities: **Wausau, Merrill, Gleason**
Fly/Bait Shop, Guide Service: **Gander Mountain**
(Wausau)

The Prairie River offers anglers 42 miles of Class I (nine miles) and Class II trout water as it winds through Langlade and Lincoln counties. Due to the removal of the long-standing Prairie Dells Dam in 1991, things may gradually get even better. Browns and brookies reproduce naturally in upper parts of the river. There is some stocking of rainbows in the lower river.

The Prairie's multiple personalities make it one of those rivers that offers something to suit pretty much anyone's and everyone's tastes. It is one of those stretches of water that, somewhere along its length, looks exactly like a trout stream is supposed to look, no matter who's doing the looking. Here, it's wide and rushing between tree-lined banks; there, narrow and slowly meandering through meadow. In some places, the bank slopes gently down to the water, in others it runs between steep vertical rock walls. There are spots where you can catch fish all day every day, and a couple of particularly frustrating ones where you can't catch a fish until daylight's gone.

Having said all that, it should also be noted that there are many access points along the Prairie. In general, wading is fairly easy, but there are areas that can be difficult or even treacherous, especially during high water. The latter are usually obvious, although there are a few places where the wading doesn't look like it'll be too tough until you step into the water and start slipping and tripping on the greasy cobble and rock shelf bottom.

At my favorite place on the Prairie, you stumble as gracefully as possible down a steep bank, then wade into the fast-moving water where slick rocks of every size and

Whitewater rodeo play on
Wausau's world-class Wisconsin River paddle venue.

Brachycentrus *larva American grannom.*

description challenge you to stay afoot. Once you have managed to find a position to fix yourself against the current or in an eddie behind a big boulder, while falling neither on your head nor your ass, you pause to look around at the gorgeous scenery that made the whole effort worthwhile. Since this is the perfect place to throw long casts with streamers to big trout holding in the numerous seams, you may also be rewarded with a memorable fight. (Of course, when it's all over, you do have to make that long, unpleasant and potentially hazardous wade back to shore: A trek best made prior to full dark.)

Bugs and Other Trout Food

Each of the most typical trout stream insects is represented on the Prairie, as are a nice variety of terrestrials and meat. As on almost any stream in Wisconsin, most of your nymphing needs can be met with a mix of beadhead and plain Pheasant Tails, Gold or Silver Ribbed Hare's Ears, Tan and Green Caddis, and Prince Nymphs. Throw in a couple of March Browns for good measure. Except for the caddis patterns, where you may want to go a little smaller, carry all of the above in size #12-16.

Dry-fly fishing on the Prairie will largely mirror that of the Wolf: Hendricksons, March browns and Sulphurs in #14-16;

brown drakes and mahogany duns in #12-14; white flies (White Wulffs/White Wolfs)—a potential super hatch—#12; blue-winged olives #16-18; and tiny blue-winged olives in #20-22. Naturally, you will want some small Adams; as well as the most basic of the basics, Griffith's Gnats, Bivisibles and Renegades in #14-18.

One form or another of caddis will almost always be present during the warm months. I've had good luck with Tiny Black Caddis and Deer Hairs with both tan and lime green bodies.

For stonefly patterns, you might have luck on anything from a #2-4 Salmonfly to a #16 Little Yellow Sally. Or you could try going down the middle with a #10-14 yellow or orange-thoraxed Montana Nymph.

From the meat menu, a minimalist Prairie selection could be made up of Muddlers, Little Brook and Little Brown Trout, Woolly Buggers in olive, black, brown or combinations thereof and Olive Scuds. One pattern that seems to work quite often when others don't is the Bi-Bugger developed by Rich Osthoff. (As an aside, the Bi-Bugger could be considered a Wisconsin standard since it often works everywhere when nothing else will.)

And when it comes to terrestrials, make sure you carry a couple of nice, big, juicy spider patterns for the wooded areas where the river is narrow and branches overhang from both sides to form a canopy. When you've just stuck your face into the web of one of these hairy critters, they look big and mean enough to eat mice. One can only assume, therefore, that they make great trout food.

Also from the terrestrial families, both large and small hopper, cricket, beetle, jassid and ant imitations should find success when those insects are out and about. If you like to fish with ants, carry patterns ranging in size from 14-20.

Finding Your Way

By catching Highway 17 just east of Merrill and heading north, you will more or less track the Prairie River upstream. Highway 17 crosses the Prairie and is crossed itself by a number of county and town roads offering good to excellent river access.

Food, Lodging, Entertainment

There are any number of taverns, cafes, campgrounds and motels not far from the Prairie, but the nearest community of any true size is Wausau, a few miles south. Wausau is a little city that has very nicely dealt with the problem of growing into itself. In addition to having an excellent variety of eat and drink and dance and sleep establishments, there are some other attractions well worth making a side-trip for.

During the summer, Wausau hosts several fast-water paddling events on a world-class whitewater course that runs right through the downtown. In late August every year, the Big Bull Falls Blues Festival takes place on Fern Island. The Leigh Yawkey Woodson Art Museum collects and exhibits "art of the natural world" with an emphasis on depictions of birds. The internationally known "Birds in Art" exhibit premieres the weekend after Labor Day at the museum. And the restored Grand Theater hosts a mixed calendar of music, drama and other entertainment events.

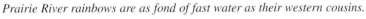

Prairie River rainbows are as fond of fast water as their western cousins.

An all-green day on the Prairie.

Northeast

Brule River

Counties: **Florence, Forest**
Nearest Communities: **Florence, Iron River**
Fly/Bait Shop, Guide Service: **Eagle Sport Center**
(Eagle River)**; We Tie It** (Boulder Junction)

There is understandably some confusion between the Brule River and the better known—it is safe to say *famous*—Bois Brule River in Wisconsin's upper left corner. The confusion stems from the fact that both Brules are commonly referred to as "the Brule." Their physical proximity simply adds to the confusion. An easy way to keep things straight in your own mind and the minds of those you talk rivers with is to refer to this river as the "border Brule" and the Bois Brule as simply that, the "Bois Brule."

The border Brule is called so, because it draws a portion of the line that separates Wisconsin from Michigan's Upper Peninsula. All of its roughly 50 miles, from Brule Lake in the UP to its confluence with the Menominee River, is trout stream. About 14 miles of it is Class I water, the remainder Class II. There are native brookies and planted browns, with supposition that many browns have gone wild too and are reproducing.

If you want to fish alone, the Brule is a good choice. Maybe it's only coincidence, but I don't recall a single trip when I encountered more than the occasional other fisher. For

Late in the day on a wide, shallow stretch of the Brule.

the most part I was alone, quite alone—in a couple of instances, disconcertingly alone. From the Wisconsin side of the Brule, there are two places I've fished where the road (if you want to call a two-track trail of that sort a road) comes to an end at river's edge. At both I was treated to a spectacular evening rise, but at the same time rattled by the sound of a thing larger than I coming through the brush in my general direction. In one of those cases, something did enter the water just around the bend, but I didn't go to see what it was. If it had only been a deer, I would have been disappointed in both it and myself.

Much of the Brule is wide—40 feet and more across—and relatively slow moving. While wading doesn't need to be difficult, you do have to take care to avoid too suddenly finding some of the river's deep holes, underwater tree snags and dead wood. And deep *does* mean deep; the kind of deep that big trout love, but fishers who prefer to stay dry and undrowned best keep out of. The bottom is mostly sand and gravel.

Along much of its length, the banks are tree-lined, often heavily forested. There are occasional open stretches, however. I had great fun on one trip sitting on the rocks above the river spotting fish for my partner casting below. In this way, she took a couple of pretty little brookies in full spawning regalia.

Elk or Deer Hair Caddis all the way from #12 to a #16 can be a good bet for surface fishing, as can ant and beetle imitations. When nymphing, experiment with Hare's Ears, Pheasant Tails, or even Soft Hackle Woolly Worms. In the deepest holes, you're most likely to hook up with a big fish by putting a streamer deep and retrieving it slow. Try a Sculpin, Muddler Minnow or an olive and black Woolly Bugger with a hint of flash.

Getting There, Being There

If you like camping, you'll find some very nice state and federal sites on both sides of the river. There's a particularly nice one right before Highway 55/73 crosses into Upper Michigan. Numerous National Forest campsites are within easy driving distance; a few on the banks of nearby trout streams. If you like to sleep and eat indoors, you'll find the greatest variety in Florence or across the border in Iron River, Michigan. Main highway river crossings are at 55/73, 189 and 2/141.

Anyone who has given thought to hunting muskie or big pike with a fly may want to check out the still water of northeastern Wisconsin. When it comes to stalking our most toothsome fishes, this is the place to be. Make a side trip to Bill Sherer's We Tie It shop in Boulder Junction for expert advice on any of the waters in the area. Or call *well* ahead, and book a trip with master angler Sherer himself. A weekend of vacation, well timed, in this area could have you putting all your rods to the test; out for muskie in the morning, panfish at midday and native brookies in the evening. And within reasonable driving distance is brown, steelhead and salmon fishing in the Great Lakes tribs.

A tie-dyed angler casts the slow water for Brule brookies.

Northeast
Pike, Pine and Popple Rivers

Counties: **Florence, Forest, Marinette**
Nearest Communities: **Florence, Pembine, Norway**

Before I first came to Wisconsin's "waterfall country," I was unaware that such things even existed here. I knew our fast water, I knew "North." But, somehow, the idea that here in the Badger State we had places where water fell in such spectacular fashion had, to that point, escaped me. I don't know how I missed them, I just did, okay?

I'd been talking to a publisher I worked with at the time about the possibility of a story on the Peshtigo Fire tragedy. His thoughts were that such a story might have some socially redeeming value, but a story on Wisconsin's waterfalls—"in the same area as Peshtigo"— would be much more palatable (read "cheery") to *our* readers. Being a young man lusting after the sight of my own words in print, I agreed to do the story his way. It didn't seem to be a good idea at the time to mention that I didn't have the slightest idea what he was talking about. (Hungry young writers are like hungry young actors: If you're asked if you can play piano for a part, you say yes and learn to play the thing before shooting starts.) I figured if my publisher already knew there were waterfalls in Wisconsin worth writing about, I could find them. And so I set out....

That was a long time ago.

I found the waterfalls. I found that each served as foamy white punctuation to a northeastern Wisconsin trout stream. Three of the trout streams of the area—the Pike, Pine and Popple—hold the distinction of being the first rivers in the United States designated by Congress as "Wild and Scenic." The designation is a good thing: It has kept these rivers truly unique. Some of us quietly (some of us sometimes not so quietly) wish that certain kinds of "improvements" could be applied, but it really is tough to argue the point when so little anymore is allowed to remain in its natural state.

While the waterfalls you will encounter on a trip to fish the Pike, Pine and Popple are mainly in Marinette County, the streams themselves weave a complex pattern across three other counties on their way to the Menominee River; Florence, Forest and Langlade. The landscape here is exactly what many of us picture when someone says "up north." Dense forest, tamarack swamps, aspen stands, blackberry brush, veritable clouds of mosquitoes, marching armies of ticks, dirt roads and, very often, the sense that you are quite alone. Yes, there *are* bears.

Once you're out of sight of whatever passed for a road where you left your vehicle, a feeling overtakes you that if something were to happen out here, something bad, you could be in big trouble, and help might not arrive anytime soon. But, of course, this is one of the things we go looking for when we leave the beaten path behind, isn't it? (If you hadn't already guessed, the partridge and woodcock hunting around these parts can be excellent.)

Stream access varies from easy to so damn difficult you have to wonder if it's worth it. You can get in at a number of bridge crossings, sometimes, in fact, directly into trout-rich little stretches of water. In other places there are designated parking areas with trails of a sort leading to the stream. Do be forewarned that, while some of these walks are short, others are likely to make you feel like Hansel or Gretel fresh out of bread crumbs. There are any number of "access points" in the area that will cause you to put serious thought into how much work fishing ought to be. In Marinette County, developed access to some of the waterfalls and a couple of parks provide the best opportunity for anglers who have difficulty with some of the more challenging geography. Another option for those so equipped, is canoeing prime-looking stretches. (If you are a novice paddler, exercise caution: These are *wild* rivers.)

As an aside, in addition to the rivers we're talking about here, many other creeks and streams of the area do harbor trout populations. And the lakes and ponds of the area hold a veritable buffet of warmwater species.

The trout are native brookies, a mix of wild and (some) planted browns and, according to others—although you couldn't prove it by me—some rainbows. In the days of heavier stocking there were rainbows in these and many other Wisconsin waters, to be sure, but those days have passed or are passing. Wisconsin's wild-trout program is well under way. With luck and the cooperation of all involved, we are moving in the most positive direction we possibly could.

There have been reports of some outsize trout, including larger than average brookies. One trip to the northeastern corner was precipitated by a very believable account of a weekend spent catching numerous brook trout in the 12- to 14-inch range. Who wouldn't be tempted to go looking for a place such as this?

The directions to the exact stretch of water where these big fish were caught sounded very detailed in the telling. Once we used them to find the spot, however, they turned out to be the kind of thing master bullshitters have been tormenting the rest of us with for years. Which is to say we put on nearly as many miles driving in circles in the stream's vicinity as we did driving the three hours from home to get there. Eventually, we

Some of the best places to fish on the Pike are also the prettiest.

Northeast: Pike, Pine and Popple Rivers

found what we were positive was the charmed water we had been directed to. From bank to bank, it was a good three feet wide, with maybe another three feet (or more!) of undercut (on each side!). Depth appeared to be between three and five feet. We wondered how anyone managed to fly-fish here. Then we remembered that the guy who told us about this place never did say anything about *fly* fishing...

Pike River

For a first-time visit, I recommend concentrating on the Pike River. Of the three, it offers the best access, the most stable flows and temperatures, the most non-fishing attractions and, some would say, the best fishing. The water might be described as classic-with-a-twist. Instead of the usual riffle-run-pool configuration, you get riffle-run-glide-falls-plunge pool-pool-flat. In wadable areas, the Pike is a freestone stream with a postcard-perfect combination of cobble, big rocks, boulders and smooth gray fallen branches surrounded by green; green everywhere. Fishing both immediately above and immediately below the falls can be superb. If you are able, you will want to hike up from your start point where there will be greater challenges and, on the best days, greater rewards. There are also bridge crossings where there are great riffle-run-riffle sections (with boulders, and therefore eddies) that can offer great fun fishing for beautiful little brookies in water the color of root beer.

Pine and Popple Rivers

The Pine sometimes seems to go ever on, twisting, turning across Florence, Forest and Langlade counties with public access at a number of road crossings. Along its length, there are some 48 miles of Class II trout water and 36 miles of Class III.

The Popple is a freehand scribble of stream through Florence and Forest counties. Roughly 24 miles of Class II water, 35 miles of Class III and a dandy mile and a half of Class I. Here too, public access is relatively plentiful.

The trout are a mix of native brookies and planted browns (although some of those browns do look like they've got a couple of years in the stream under their gills). Many of the fish, for all their splash of color, are diminutive, but skill and patience, mixed with a large, healthy dose of luck will occasionally yield a trout of remarkable size. Overall, the brook trout fishing is outstanding; the brown trout fishing is sporadically amazing.

The trick here is to bring a short rod and a mosquito-proof sense of humor.

What to Fish With

You will find some of the standard upper Midwestern hatches on the Pike, Pine and Popple, but generally not in huge numbers. Pale morning duns and Sulphers will have their days, as will both varieties of blue-winged olives. There will be some little yellow stones in late spring and early summer, and a few orange stones in mid-summer. Caddis in a variety of

Fishing the Pine in autumn,
where a brookie sits in almost every seam.

styles and colors ranging from slate gray to light tan are always good to have in your box. If you have no Upland Caddis patterns, this would be a good time to get some. Nymph fishing on these streams would get mixed reviews from me (until I find the one that nails 'em, that is). Streamers are another story. Little Brook Trout, Little Brown Trout, Thunder Creeks and Mickey Finns can all turn a trout's eye on the right day.

This is one of those areas where matching anything exactly is often of minor concern. Carry a good stock of Adams, Royal and Ausable Wulffs, Irresistibles, Warden's Worries and Woolly Buggers, along with a few of the flies listed above, and you'll be in good shape.

Getting There

For the most part, you will *not* find the Pike, Pine or Popple crowded. Along with your *Wisconsin Atlas & Gazetteer*, you should have Florence, Forest, Langlade and Marinette county maps. These rivers weave complex patterns across their counties, and unless you are on an extended vacation, you probably want to tackle them one at a time. As a general guide, when on the Pike, Pine or Popple, you will be west of Highway 141, south of Highway 70 and both north and south of Highway 8.

Low water on the Popple, minutes before a heavy rain.

Food and Lodging

When it comes to food and lodging, keep one thing in mind, you are here to fish. If you are a picky eater or have very specific tastes or needs, carry along your own food and a portable grill. I've yet to find any area in Wisconsin that doesn't have at least one *great* place to eat; I just haven't found it yet up here. I've stumbled on some pretty good bar burgers, and you can always find a pizza of sorts. Pasties (a vegetable-and-meat-filled Welsh/Cornish pastry) are a local favorite, but my personal opinion is that they are an overrated tribute to bland and not worth the time it takes to bake them. For the greatest variety, cross the border to Iron Mountain or Norway, Michigan. Don't get in too late, or you'll find the sidewalks have been rolled up before your arrival.

For lodging, we can make two strong recommendations. Do be encouraged, however, to either make reservations or be ready to sleep in your vehicle. The Grand Motel in Pembine is a terrific little mom and pop shop, replete with fine folk running the place. And thanks to the brother of those fine folk who happened to be motel-sitting the first time we stopped there looking for lodging (without reservations), we were directed to the Viking Motel in Norway, Michigan, and we were *very* pleased. Campers should have no problem finding a place to pitch their tents. There are a number of parks that offer camping. And Nicolet National Forest is an outdoors person's dream, replete with trout streams, fish-full little lakes and some damn fine grouse hunting.

Attractions

Naturally, you would be remiss if you didn't visit at least a couple of the northeast's waterfalls. Get a copy of the Marinette County "Waterfalls Capital" brochure (available at many stops in the area or from Marinette County Tourism, Box 320 WF, Marinette, WI 54143.) You will also find the area well-suited to antique hunting, and there are a couple of unique museums.

If you're up to a hard dose of cold reality, visit the museum and cemetery in Peshtigo, and give a few seconds of sad quiet to the victims of a terrible moment in Wisconsin history. When you hear voices in the middle of a waterfall country night, this is one of the places from which they come.

Peshtigo River

Counties: **Marinette, Forest**
Nearest Communities: **Peshtigo, Marinette, Crivitz**
Fly/Bait Shop, Guide Service: **Bob's Bait & Tackle**
(Green Bay)**; Nickolai Sporting Goods** (Green Bay)

Opinions vary as to how much of the Peshtigo River is trout water. One WDNR publication ranks over 70 miles of the river as Class II. Other less official, but usually reliable, sources estimate between 30 and 50 miles. Two things are certain: The Peshtigo is a long river; and much of it holds trout. In fact, the lowest reaches of the Peshtigo even offer anglers the chance to dance with steelhead, lake-run browns and chinook salmon.

At least part of the reason there is a discrepancy between reports on exactly how much of the Peshtigo is actually trout water is that it is a river that *looks* like it should hold a great deal more fish than it does. That isn't to say the fishing isn't good, it's only to say that it isn't as good some times some places as it is others. And when it's not good, the fish can be very, very difficult to find.

Caddis pupa.

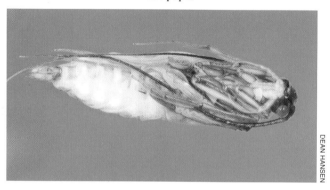

The problem lies largely in temperature variances that are not conducive to large, stable trout populations. Due, however, to a population of highly productive beavers that is large *and* stable, many of the Peshtigo's tributaries are dammed. (Interesting to note here, perhaps, how dammed so often becomes damned.) This causes summer water temperatures throughout the Peshtigo system, including the main river, to rise to *uncomfortable* levels, and winter temperatures to drop well below what they need to be. Beaver dam removal is regularly practiced on Wisconsin streams, but our limited human resources would have to be much busier than beavers to keep up. Trout, especially wild trout, tend to move around, and with big variances in water temperatures, they move even more, looking for water that meets their needs. The result: Long stretches of water may be full of fish or fish-free depending on the season.

Hendrickson Ephemerella subvaria.

It is only fair to report that Man, more in the quest for power than from a need to be beaver-like, has also placed a series of dams on the Peshtigo. And they are *not* managed to create the kind of excellent tailwater fishery as is the case in some other states.

What this all means to the trout-fisher is relatively simple: Fish the undammed upper river during cool or moderate weather, and fish another river entirely during summer temperature peaks. By following these rules, you'll find the fish plentiful and the fishing good. It may be so good that the river even fools you into thinking it is fishing as good as it looks like it should.

Certainly on warm days, but at other times as well, fish the fast water and the edges to find the highest degree of success. These are the places where the trout are going to hold during all but absolutely perfect conditions and large hatches. If you are good at dropping or drifting a fly at the edge of the bank so fish hiding in the undercut can see it go by, you have an advantage. If you know how to lay a fly across multiple currents and stacked riffles without a hint of drag, you should do well.

Considering the inaccessibility of much of the surrounding area, accessibility to the river itself is pretty good. If you're willing to do some hiking (not necessarily easy hiking), your options are even greater. Some of the more dramatic sections of the Peshtigo do an excellent job of reminding you that you are alive—sometimes by making it ultimately clear that you may not be for long. Ask any whitewater kayaker and he or she will tell you that, when the water is at its best (or is it worst?), the experience is invigorating to say the very least. Fishing the Peshtigo (and the Wolf and the Bois Brule) made my first step into rivers like the Gallatin, Fryingpan and other western waters with occasionally nasty dispositions a much more manageable experience. The hike in, while certainly not threatening in the same way, can also put your motivations to test.

If you like short walks, or better yet parking next to the piece of water you will fish, you will still find a variety of fine accesses on the Peshtigo, but you may also encounter more competition than on the less accessible waters. There are a couple of parks on the Peshtigo that you will *not* be able to see without stopping to fish. Accessibility here is great, but the only way you're going to have a pool to yourself is to arrive in the middle of the week, and even then, well...

Goodman County Park and McClintock County Park are separated by only a few miles, Goodman being the northern-most (and perhaps the prettier) of the two. Both offer a variety of excellent angling opportunities, through generally fast-moving water with waterfalls, rapids and riffles. Both are also excellent rest and picnic sites. If you stop at either of these parks at season's end, or in winter, you may be fooled into thinking you have found a great secret place, but take my word for it, the secret was out a long time ago.

How to Fish the Peshtigo

For the most part, you can find success on the Peshtigo by following the recommendations given earlier for fishing the Wolf. One method that seems to work particularly well in wide, riffle sections of the river with numerous small boulders, is short-line nymphing. And, because of the broken surface, you can get by with a 5X, or sometimes even a 4X, tippet to make up a little for the high stick and the minimum of line out past the tip. If you aren't used to fishing this way, you may break off a few times before you get the hang of it, but it's a technique worth learning; and one that will stand you well in fast water from one end of the country to the other. Experiment with everything from big Soft Hackle Woolly Worms to mid-size Pheasant Tails and Hare's Ears, all the way down to tiny Sow Bugs.

Finding Your Way

Draw a rectangle with the Bay of Green Bay and Highway 41 on its right edge, Highway 32 on its left, Highway 64 at its bottom and Highway 8 at its top. Within this somewhat mis-shapen box flows the Peshtigo, as well as a handful of little streams, plus some lakes and ponds, that harbor trout and a number of warmwater species. Numerous County and Forest roads will provide access to these treasures.

Late season on the Peshtigo is neither the time nor the place for sissies.

Northeast

Oconto River

Counties: **Oconto, Langlade**
Nearest Communities: **Oconto, Stiles, Oconto Falls,**
    Shawano
Fly/Bait Shop, Guide Service: **Bob's Bait & Tackle**
    (Green Bay)**; Nickolai Sporting Goods** (Green Bay)

It's a large river; a river *system*. It is a spider web of prime trout water that radiates across its corner of northeastern Wisconsin. It *owns* that part of the state through which flows. If you are at its center, there is no direction you can go without crossing it several times. At one end, it's crowded with Technicolor little brookies, at the other a tailwater populated by trout and salmon that might truly be as long as your leg (or at least as big around). I know a couple of 100-day-a-year guys who find it hard to tear themselves away from the Oconto to fish anywhere else. One of them told me—with perhaps the slightest hint of exaggeration—that he couldn't plan his annual two weeks in Montana, because he had to go "when the fish aren't biting on the Oconto."

For our purposes, we can look at the Oconto as two unique entities: The upper river and its many tributaries where wild brookies and browns share the water with some planted browns and rainbows; and the lower river, from the Stiles dam to Green Bay in the city (little—real little—city) of Oconto, where chinook salmon, three strains of steelhead (Skamania, Chambers Creek and Ganaraska), lake-run browns, walleyes, smallmouth bass and panfish can all be found, depending on when you're out. It's easy to see how someone who knows the river could feel the Oconto is enough.

The Oconto has over 100 miles of trout water. More than 50 miles of it is Class I. As with many Wisconsin trout streams, regulations vary throughout the Oconto system. The idea of establishing the regulations to fit each stream, or to apply different regs to different parts of the same stream have been very good for Wisconsin fish and fishers. The positive effects can be seen across the state. However, as with all things, there is always something new to be learned.

There is a catch to our five-category trout regs that came to light as the result of studies performed on the upper Oconto in the early '90s. Our regs are based on the idea that by placing additional restraints on equipment and harvest in a given stretch of water, we will grow either larger or more trout. The problem is, or may be, that these special-regs stretches of water are usually fairly short in length. The Oconto studies used tagging and radio transmitters to track trout movements. What they found was that while some trout do stay within a relatively limited area, others travel considerable distances: As much as 30 miles! More recent supposition argues that trout may even travel considerably farther than that, depending on water conditions. There is some discussion concerning these long pilgrimages, but the general consensus

is that the culprit is water temperature. Once the water reaches about 60 degrees, the trout head for cooler climes.

Obviously, this means that trout are somewhat protected as long as they are in special-regs water, but the chances of them being there depend largely on the temperature of the day. It is possible and likely that on hot summer days, trout of remarkable size may be taken (and kept) where people often go to catch a handful of small, breakfast brookies. We all know that when the weather warms, trout head for cool places, so why not cool places far from where we normally expect to find them?

Wisconsin continues to review and evaluate its fishing regulations with resource and user in mind. The likelihood is high that regs will change as we learn more and become more skilled at protecting *and* managing the resource. In the meantime, it is up to us to find the trout wherever they may be. That is, after all, a large part of what this is all about isn't it?

The Upper River

The branches of the upper Oconto may be thought of as quite tree-like, until you take into account the minor tributaries that often also hold fish. Then the spider-web image seems more appropriate. You might fish the North Branch, the First South Branch, the Second South Branch, the South Branch or even the main river where all these flows become one. Virtually all of it holds trout, although some of it is much more accessible than the rest. And there are a couple of miles of the Oconto that flow through the northeast corner of the Menominee Indian Reservation (Menominee County) where public fishing is prohibited.

While there are some dandy fishing, floating, canoeing, camping spots along the North Branch in the Nicolet National Forest (much of the river runs through the Forest), my personal favorite places to fish the Oconto are at a couple select stops between the northern border of Menominee County and Highway 64, and just east of Menominee County between County Highway AA on the north and State Highway 32 on the east. The latter of the two strikes me as most conducive to fly-fishing...and most likely to turn up large fish. (Note here that the average fish you catch anywhere on the upper Oconto may be between 10 and 14 inches, but there are a number of known catches of fish over 20 inches throughout the system.)

What you fish with here, as well as how you fish, may be guided by the lures, gear and techniques recommended for other northeastern streams. A pair of notable variances are worth mentioning.

First, I have never fished another Wisconsin stream where I have seen caddis hatches as prodigious as those on this river. It may be coincidental to when I've been there, but you won't find me on the Oconto without a selection of Elk Hair Caddis from size 12 to 6, along with a mix of other types and sizes of caddis and caddis emerger patterns.

Second, in *Exploring Wisconsin Trout Streams: The Angler's Guide*, the authors make thinly veiled reference to cronies (or a crony) of theirs from the Madison area who fish(es), it would seem, almost exclusively with the Wisconsin originated Pass Lake dry-fly pattern. They remark on the good fortune this favorite fly has often attracted on the Oconto. In hopes of improving my record there, I have sought out the advice of two anglers of my own acquaintance who often fish the Oconto and found that they, too, made the Pass Lake their first choice. So, no matter what the time of year, no matter what the time of day, it shouldn't be too hard to figure out what the first fly I tie on will be, if there's nothing obvious in the air or on the surface.

The Lower River

From the 1890s to the early 1980s, the lower Oconto River was one of the most polluted waterways in Wisconsin. The culprit was typically careless paper mill processes. What turned things around was that, for a change, the bad guys lost, really lost; perhaps not as much as they should have, but enough to make a difference. The offending mill, located in Oconto Falls, was cited for non-compliance and Scott Paper, the company that operated it, was sued by the WDNR and US EPA in 1977. The mill was closed in February 1978. A year later, in January 1979, Scott settled out of court with a $1,000,000 "forfeiture;" $600,000 of which was earmarked for the DNR to come up with a plan to restore portions of the river and Green Bay, damaged by mill discharges. In 1984, the DNR began stocking steelhead in the Oconto and at its mouth in Green Bay. Success with steelhead stocking was followed by the addition of brown trout and chinook salmon.

The lower Oconto was well on its way to recovery when a second important development took place in the early 1990s. At that time, the WDNR and the US Fish and Wildlife Service reached an agreement with Oconto Electric Cooperative, operator of a hydroelectric dam at Stiles, which resulted in more stable flows and a healthier aquatic environment.

With the three strains of steelhead, plus the lake run browns and salmon, the stretch of river between the Stiles dam at Highway 141 and Green Bay provides nearly year-round fishing for salmonids. (Occasionally even a brookie or lake trout will move into the river from the bay.) Steelhead come into the river in early spring, mid-summer and late fall. Browns swim up in fall and down in spring when the water warms. The chinooks also make their upstream run in fall. Combined with the warmwater species available, this can make for a wonderfully varied fishing experience.

A productive piece of stream if patience and skill prevail.

Lures for the Lower River

When deciding what the fly of choice should be for prospecting (or sight-fishing) the lower Oconto, or any stream dumping into Green Bay or Lake Michigan, you can go anywhere from simple to complex, with several choices in between. If you watch the bait guys, you'll see a lot of spawn sacs being tossed into deep runs. There is no reason not to start here yourself. Any egg pattern in orange, red, pink or combinations thereof could be deadly. Orange with just the slightest amount of yellow or red mixed in makes an interesting lure. If basic egg patterns are a little too close to bait for you, either an Egg Sucking Leech or a Double Butt Glitter Bitch can be a fine alternative, allowing you to feel more like you're fishing with a fly and still presenting the fish with something that looks like spawn.

Woolly Buggers or other leech imitations in black, purple, gray, white, chartreuse or pink are commonly used on Oconto trout and salmon. Also popular with a few fishers are some of the more simple Atlantic and Pacific salmon fly and streamer patterns in black or bright colors, with flash. If you are lucky enough to intercept browns on their way back to the bay on a day when there's a hatch, you might catch them on some of the larger mayfly and stonefly nymphs, as well as basic dry-fly patterns.

Reminders of a long-gone Wisconsin.

Welcome signs to a very friendly stretch of the Oconto.

How to Fish the Lower River

Any number of techniques have been found to work on just the right day, but the one that works consistently for bait-fishers, spin-casters *and* fly-fishers almost any day is a standard across stream cast (or down-and-across, depending on your surroundings and current conditions) with the lure bouncing along (or near) the bottom and a swing at the end.

Begin by weighting your fly or line enough to ensure that it will hit bottom or float near bottom. Cast across-stream, immediately making a large upstream mend. The mend will let your fly get down deeper and help you avoid the enemy that is slack so that you can feel—or sense—the tick at the end of your tippet when a fish strikes.

A note of caution: There's some very deep water here. This is great for holding fish, but not so great for wader-clad fishers who have lost their footing.

Some of the bait guys use bobbers, and you may want to as well. Yeah, I know, we're supposed to call them strike indicators, but a bobber is a bobber is a bobber. A well-greased piece of yarn well up from your fly can work out real well and won't be as startling when it hits the surface as some of the commercial strike indicators are.

As your fly floats downstream, you will feel it bump along the bottom or briefly catch on underwater rocks and weeds. Be ready. If you see, feel or sense anything that might be a strike, set your hook. You will lose a few flies, but that's part of this kind of fishing. As your fly reaches the end of its drift, let it swing across the current toward you. This is often where the strike will occur. When your fly completes its swing, allow it to swim in the current for a second or two, then begin a slow retrieve before picking the line up and casting again.

If you are fortunate to have a piece of stream to yourself, work it diligently and hard, first across, then farther across, then down, then farther down. Be patient...and tireless. In Wisconsin, the Muskie is known as the fish of 10,000 casts, but the big trout can't be far behind.

Door County Streams

County: **Door**
Nearest Communities: **Sturgeon Bay, Jacksonport, Bailey's Harbor, Egg Harbor, Fish Creek, Sister Bay, Ellison Bay**
Fly/Bait Shop, Guide Service: **Bob's Bait & Tackle** (Green Bay)

Boats. Boats everywhere. All shapes and sizes. All colors. From sometime in April to sometime in November, Door County roads and waters are crawling with boats. Fishing boats in particular.

For the longest time, I would come to Door County on weekends, vacations and holidays and not fish. If this doesn't strike you as odd, you must understand that Door County is a peninsula sticking its mitten thumb out into the blue-green of Lake Michigan and Green Bay, and that I fish *everywhere*, *all the time*. It is rare, and a little disturbing, for me to leave home without fishing gear in the car. But each trip to Door County, at first, further convinced me that there was no point in even attempting to fish here if you didn't have a boat. And I don't have a boat.

My practice of coming here sans fishing gear changed one Independence Day weekend some years ago when my brother-in-law and his wife suggested our family join them for a few days of camping and fishing at Potawatomi State Park. They had a boat. A very small boat, to be sure, but big enough for two adults and one child to fish from in relative comfort as long as weather conditions were mild and no one moved around too much. My mental picture prior to the trip was one of me and my bro, or anyone else, spending long hours each day afloat on the sun-reflecting waters of Sturgeon Bay,

pulling in, one after another, all the fish I was sure one could catch if only one had a boat...even a very small boat. The reality was that my brother-in-law and his wife were usually out in the boat from morning 'til night, and except for a couple of hours one Saturday evening, I stayed ashore. (I *will* say that my son and daughter did get in some boat fishing over that week and both caught more fish than they ever had fishing with me in Door County. Come to think of it, so did my wife.)

The point is, I was left with plenty of gear and plenty of time with which to figure out how to fish the Door without a boat. It turned out that in Potawatomi there was a place next to a small light (navigational aid) where perch were plentiful and the prospect of an occasional smallmouth bass, or even a trout, was fairly good. And east along the shore, there was another light before which one could stand upon a large rock, throwing long casts to perch and ever-present smallmouth along the dark edge of a drop-off. Here, too, there might be a trout that would be fooled by a very patient angler. (At this site in August 1999, my four-year-old granddaughter, Nia, caught her first fish ever; a 15-inch smallmouth bass.)

Striking out from the park by car, I found that a resourceful, boatless fisher need not go fishless. A number of piers offered fair-to-excellent opportunities. In other places there were rock points where one could sit and cast. And in still others, it was

Every direction you turn in Door County is a picture waiting to be taken.

The cruel beauty at battle's end.

possible to wade out and throw a line far enough to effectively search the drop-offs where numerous fish held.

Driving along the county's east coast, I was intrigued by the small streams that feed into Lake Michigan. Of all the times I had driven across them in previous years, I never before noticed their resemblance to the northern Wisconsin trout streams my father loved so, until I crossed them with the tools of a fisher at hand. When this thought entered my mind initially, however, it was hot in early July. There was sign neither of fish nor fishers.

It was late April the following year when I gave more serious thought to Door County's Lake Michigan tributaries as a place to fish with any real purpose. (That is to say, consider them places where fish might be caught.)

I was driving south on County Q. As I came around the curve just above Moonlight Bay and Reiboldt's Creek, I was confronted by a unique sight. Along the bay, on the east side of the bridge, the marshy southern shore was dotted with fishers. Along the creek, on the west side of the road, angling was a wool plaid, shoulder-to-shoulder affair. We pulled over to more closely survey the scene. One look into the water revealed the source of all this activity. Below the surface of the shallow water, trout were everywhere.

The crowd, it so happened, was a once-in-a-decade deal. The spring steelhead run—while it may never again equal in numbers that first sighting for me—is a predictable annual event. In fact, virtually every creek along the county's east coast is a spring and fall fishing hotspot (as long as there's

One of many take-your-breath-away views from Door County landfall to big water full of trout and other species.

enough water in the creeks for the fish to get in). In fall, brown trout are accompanied on their upstream run by chinook and coho salmon. Steelhead make their appearance as spring rains and snowmelt runoff swell the streams. Brook trout (astonishingly large brook trout) are also often present.

Anyone who has done it, will quickly testify that hooking up with one of these bruisers and battling it to hand is every bit as exciting as any fishing from a boat could be. Those who do it regularly wouldn't trade it for any other fishing experience.

The fisher sneaks along the shore, bent low to avoid being caught in the trout's vision. He walks softly, knowing that heavy footsteps on the bank or stirring the water's edge will be telegraphed to the trout's ultra-sensitive lateral line where sound is felt more quickly than it could ever be heard by the human ear. The fisher's clothing is camouflage from the top of his hat to the soles of his wading boots so that he better blends with his surroundings. There are those who would say all this attention to stealth is unnecessary, that these fish will take anything you put in front of them. Their own good luck not withstanding, they are wrong. Whether you are standing on shore or in the water, your skills at arriving unseen and unheard will serve you well.

For bait-fishers, the bait of choice is the spawn of their prey. Spawn sacks are heavily preferred, though some anglers choose to fish with single eggs. Fly-fishers rely on the usual bits of yarn tied to resemble single eggs or clumps of spawn for the most part, but they also work a variety of streamers.

While one fisher may describe a steelhead's take as sudden and violent, another may recall it as subtle as a lover's

Flats fishing in Door County November.

Northeast: Door County Streams

*Bittersweet nightshade, a common streamside sight.
Look but don't eat.*

first kiss. There is nothing subtle, however, about what happens once the trout is on. Be prepared for a long, hard downstream run, your line being torn out so fast that it might burst into flames at any second. Then, just when you think the fish may be tiring, it turns and swims back towards you faster than you can get the line back onto your reel. If you are successful, the battle will end with you tailing the fish or holding a net stretched to near breaking by a specimen that may go over 30 inches and weigh 10 pounds or more.

Reiboldt's Creek is the northernmost Door stream with major runs of spawning trout. And, since much of the area along the stream is state owned, public access is excellent. Hein's Creek runs from Kangaroo Lake to Lake Michigan south of Bailey's Harbor. The next stream down is Hibbard's Creek just north of Jacksonport. Whitefish Bay Creek is where Clark Lake empties. It can be accessed from Cave Point Drive. Whitefish provides fairly easy fishing, and fishing can be good all the way up to the dam site. Stoney Creek flows into the big lake at the southeastern corner of the county. Some fishers think of Stoney Creek as the most promising Door County stream of all. *Remember*, when heading for Door County streams, that all things are dependent on sufficient water levels.

Virtually all Door County trout fishing—no matter where you do it—is the result of massive stocking on the part of

A salmon returned to the inevitable.

Wisconsin's DNR. While trout do swim upstream to spawn, county streams are not conducive to successful natural reproduction. This in no way takes away from the experience of an angler with a thrashing 12-pound, four-year-old bolt of silver at the other end of the line.

A couple of final notes. You need a Great Lakes Trout and Salmon stamp to fish for trout in Door. And, with so much Door County shoreline in private ownership and the value of privacy being what it is, you must be careful not to violate the legal rights of others. The simple fact is that some of these folks get awfully testy when strangers start wandering across their expensive little lots.

Eats, Sleeps and Entertainment

Door County may have more good-to-great places to sleep and eat than any other area in Wisconsin. The county begins as a true Midwestern treasure, but simply put, too damn many of the folks who visit there stay and open a restaurant, a B&B, a motel, a gallery, a trendy clothing store. Yes, a blessing. Yes, a curse. Depending on when you go (fortunately, the best trout fishing is before and after most of the flatlanders have departed or before they come back), peace and quiet, *and* a vacant room or campsite can be hard to find. In spring and mid- to later fall, things are pretty open, the county relatively quiet. It's hard to find a bad place to stay or a bad meal. My own preference in lodging runs from Peninsula, Potawatomi and Newport State Parks to Peninsula Motel (Fish Creek) or Wills' Bayview Cottage & Apartment in Ellison Bay. There are still mom and pop places up here that don't get the attention of some of the hotter spots but offer an atmosphere in which fisherfolk may feel more at home.

Dining in Door is like sleeping in Door: There are so many good-to-great dining options that you would have a hard time going wrong. But some of my own favorites are plain, old standards that happen to have terrific food. Begin with breakfast at the White Gull Inn (Fish Creek) or Al Johnson's (Sister Bay); for lunch, try Smilin' Bob's Barroom Chili at the Bayside Tavern (Fish Creek) or a burger at the Cornerstone (Sister Bay); dinner could take you back to the White Gull, Voight's (Ellison Bay) or the Cookery (Fish Creek), but if it's Friday night, you have to order up the perch fry at the Sister Bay Bowl (yes, do bring your ball; it *is* a bowling alley).

After dinner, head out to the AC Tap (between Sister Bay and Bailey's Harbor) for beer, beanbag toss and an eclectic boom box selection of the bartender's favorite tunes, or go for some "danceable" rock & roll at one of the local clubs. A handful of nightspots offer a mix of rock, blues, jazz and folk music both in and out of season.

Galleries abound. Shops abound. Candy stores abound. Door County is a place that will re-educate you on how to spend your money if you happen to have forgotten. But come at the right time, find your own pace and space, and it's a wonderful place to lay low and fish for a few days.

Sandhill cranes are common company to the Badger fly-fisher.

East Coast

Counties: **Kewaunee, Manitowoc, Sheboygan**
Nearest Communities: **Algoma, Kewaunee, Two Rivers, Manitowoc, Sheboygan**
Fly/Bait Shop, Guide Service: **Bob's Bait & Tackle** (Green Bay)**; Nickolai Sporting Goods** (Green Bay)

The history of big lake-dwelling trout in Wisconsin begins with Lake Michigan's lake trout and the native lake, coaster brook trout and steelhead of Lake Superior. (The coasters and steelhead, of course, both being lake-run trout that head up into the tributaries to spawn.) A terrific combination for fishers seeking the largest of the North American trouts. Thanks, however, to overharvest of the resource and foreign invaders, the coasters are virtually gone, the wild steelhead exist in considerably smaller numbers (and only on the state's north coast) and native lake trout, while apparently reproducing naturally in Lake Superior, are little more than a memory on Lake Michigan.

But in spite of commercial fishermen, alewives, sea lampreys and zebra mussels, to say nothing of pollution and dramatic fluctuations in water levels and temperatures, Wisconsin still has a terrific "big trout" fishery. The key to this phenomenon is stocking. As the Badger steers toward a dream of an all-wild trout population, this is one place where stocking has contributed to the survival of the entire fishery (both trout and non-trout fish, as well as the environment itself, have benefited), and the practice is expected to continue well into the future.

As in the Bois Brule and a few other Lake Superior tributaries, there very likely is some natural reproduction in the Kewaunee River, where, once past the weirs, trout and salmon have some 20 miles of stream to make home. As they swim into the weirs, many fish are stripped of their eggs, then put back into the river. Others are allowed to continue their upstream journey. Most of the Lake Michigan streams are incapable of sustaining naturally reproducing trout and salmon populations. There is simply too much fluctuation in water levels and temperatures.

Great Lakes stocking was first recorded in the late 1800s, but it was in the 1960s that our modern stocking programs

Deer are common virtually everywhere in Wisconsin.

started. Stocking efforts that began with a few thousand steelhead in the early '60s have grown to incredible proportions, with several million fish currently stocked each year. Those fish include several strains of steelhead, plus browns, brookies and salmon. In addition to such benefits as control of alewives (nasty little smelt-like fishes that otherwise end up dead in stinking, rotting layers on Lake Michigan beaches), both big-water and tributary fishing have had a *very* positive effect on the local economies of lakeside villages.

The sheer volume of trout running up the Kewaunee throughout the year is reason enough to begin your search for Wisconsin steelhead and salmon there. If you fish below the collection station, you are likely to have company. It is a place where, on good days, you will find trout and/or salmon in large numbers and the fishing (once you find a place of your own) easy. Note that I said the *fishing* was easy, *not* the catching. Above the collection station, the fish may be spread out more and even harder to catch, but you are more likely to have a stretch of river all to yourself.

Other East Coast Streams

Virtually any river or creek that empties into Lake Michigan is a likely candidate for steelhead or salmon runs. It's an amazement sometimes: One day you are fishing to crowds of migrating fish on a little stream running high and fresh with spring rains, and on another, that same stream is blocked from

the big lake by a sand bar a hundred feet long due to a dry autumn; the stream above the lake holding just a trickle of water to remind you and itself that it is indeed alive.

Among the most dependable and popular east coast anadromous trout streams are the Manitowoc, Pigeon and Sheboygan. All are great streams running through woods and farm country down to the fishing villages where they empty into Lake Michigan. Of course those fishing villages depend on a great deal more than fishing to keep going these days, but trout and salmon are very much a part of what keeps them as healthy as they are.

If I have a favorite among the group—after the Kewaunee—it would be the Pigeon. My preference leans heavily toward inland trout fishing, even if the fish aren't as big, and this is, to me at least, the big fish stream that offers the closest thing to my preferred setting. And, it is a stream on which I'm often able to find a place to be alone.

Another fellow I've tested the water with swears allegiance to the Sheboygan. I like fishing the Sheboygan (when I can find a place to stand among the other flailing fishers of every cut and stripe), but my luck there has been so-so at best. I've watched my partner pull in one steelie after another while I, and everyone else, went fishless. I've even tried to fish the exact same lure and method at his side like a shameless copycat (because that's what I was) and come a cropper: Maybe that's one reason I don't care much for the guy.

Hook-up on the Kewaunee on a snowless December day.

How And What To Fish

The method that seems to yield the most success, when there's room to apply it, is across-and-down. Cast straight across or slightly down from your position. Make a big upstream mend, or two, to allow your fly to sink and to help prevent drag. Do *not* allow your line to form a belly. You want to feel, see or sense even the most subtle strike. As your line reaches the end of its drift, allow it to make a complete swing through. Begin stripping just prior to the end of the swing. Pick up, cast, repeat. After you've drifted a line through a couple of times, let out another foot or two and go through the whole process again.

Hoppers are always a favorite with hungry trout.

You won't be catching a lot of big trout and salmon on dry flies. (If you do, please give me a call: I'd like to take lessons. Yes, I *will* pay.) The typical approach on these streams is to use sinking lines, sink-tips, lead, weighted flies or any combination of the above (including a combination of all of them), with bead and cone heads thrown in for good measure. Since I like to fish with floating lines, my own approach is usually to use a well-weighted fly, or a sinking-tip, or lead, tin or tungsten not too far up from the fly. The fact is, I just hate dealing with full-sink lines on moving water. A light application of one of the commercial liquid sinkers, such as Xink, doesn't hurt either. You can probably see why this kind of fishing is called "chuck and duck."

Set aside any aversion you have to bait-fishing, and begin your fly selection with anything that looks like an egg or egg cluster in yellow, chartreuse, pink, orange or red. (For fun, and simplicity's sake, add a strike indicator—yes, a bobber—at the point where line and leader connect instead of farther down on the leader.) Egg imitations are effective. It doesn't pay to argue the point. If, however, you must fish with something less "crude" than the above, consider a Woolly Bugger in any of the aforementioned colors—purple, black, silver or white—with a little Flashabou thrown in for good measure. Leeches can also be a good choice (as long as there's a little purple and a little flash). From there, move to streamers using

The entrance to the collection facility at Kewaunee celebrates both fish and a man.

some of the same colors and combinations. Should you want to go a bit more exotic, try Kelly Galloup's Zoo Cougar. Kelly is the owner of the Troutsman fly shop in Traverse City, Michigan, and he's had plenty of experience with big trout. The Zoo Cougar comes highly recommended by a couple of trusted Michigan *and* Wisconsin fly-fishers. If you want to go even a bit more exotic, try a Double Butt Glitter Bitch. This is a pattern that was passed to me by a stranger, in the dark, over beers, outside a mom and pop motel in eastern Wyoming a few years back, and it does have all the earmarks of a great steelhead fly: Big hook, maybe size 4 or even 2; bright orange yarn ball at either end, and gold, silver, green and red glitter (flash) along the shank. It's hard to tell whether it looks more like the enemy or a cheap date to a trout, but it works.

You Can't Fish 24 Hours a Day

From the tail end of Door County to Milwaukee, Wisconsin's east coast offers a fantastic variety of places to see, things to do, places to stay, places to eat and places to be quiet. A call, a letter or an e-mail to the Department of Tourism will hook you up with a long list of possibilities. My personal favorites include: Camping, hiking, swimming, picnicking, pretty much anything at Point Beach State Park just north of Two Rivers; lunch at Kurtz's in Two Rivers; a slow walk around Rogers Fishing Village in Two Rivers; a hot fudge sundae with cashews at Berentsen's in Manitowoc; a coastal hot air balloon ride; a visit to the Maritime Museum, including the submarine tour, in Manitowoc; any meal, or drinks and talk at the Horse & Plow in Kohler; dinner at Smith Brothers in Port Washington; walks on the pier at any of the villages along the lake. Basically, this is a difficult place not to have a good time.

Getting there

The most simple approach to exploring the east coast up to Manitowoc is to head either north or south on Interstate 43 and swing east to the streams noted. From Manitowoc north to Algoma, Highway 42 should be the lake-hugging route of choice.

Central

Net Making Caddis

DEAN HANSEN

Blue-Winged Olive Spinner

DEAN HANSEN

Central

Tomorrow (Waupaca) River

Counties: **Waupaca, Portage**
Nearest Communities: **Waupaca,**
    Amherst, Scandinavia, Iola, Stevens Point
Fly/Bait Shop, Guide Service:
    One Stop Sport Shop (Stevens Point)

It takes one hour to get from my home in east central Wisconsin trout hell to the Tomorrow River. I envy those folks who live next to a stream and keep a rod strung next to the screen door so they can go cast a line anytime they feel like it. But lacking their good fortune, the Tomorrow in an hour ain't bad. It's a beautiful stretch of water, with plentiful fish and a full schedule of classic Midwestern hatches. I've never had a day on the Tomorrow that wasn't worth the drive.

Finding the Tomorrow

The Tomorrow is easy to find. Its headwaters are a few miles east of Stevens Point, above Highway 66, near Rosholt, in Portage County. From there it winds, wiggles and meanders its way south and east, weaving its way back and forth across Highway 10, to Waupaca where its designation as a trout stream is generally considered to end. (From Waupaca, the river continues on to its confluence with the lower Wolf.) Take note that when the river exits Portage County and enters Waupaca County, it becomes the Waupaca River. The Tomorrow and Waupaca are *not* two separate rivers as is sometimes thought.

A River's Character

The character of the Tomorrow and its surroundings change considerably from the headwaters downstream. At its upper end, it is as narrow as 10 feet across. By the time the river reaches Waupaca, its width has increased to 50 feet across in spots. The river begins in swamp, then flows through a gently undulating evergreen landscape and finally opens into farm field and meadow with a shade tree edge. Sometimes the bottom is muck, sometimes sand, sometimes it is gravel strewn with boulders. It is both spring creek and freestone stream. My personal experience is that you are more likely to catch brookies at the upper end and browns at the lower, with some overlap for the entire length.

How I fish the Tomorrow and what part I fish depends on a number of things. When only an evening is available, my tendency is to fish the Waupaca end, because it's closer to the place where I reside, and therefore quicker to get to. Unfortunately, on weekday evenings, this end of the river also attracts the most fishers, many of them having come from the same area as myself. It can be difficult on these evenings to find a place of one's own, especially if it happens to be during either the Hex or white fly hatch. On weekends, with a little patience, you can always find a good spot, but sometimes you may have to drive one bridge or pull-off farther on than you

planned. Weekday mornings and afternoons, when most of the competition is busy at work, are the best for anyone desirous of solitude. Admittedly, it's hard to equal the great evening hatches, but the fishing can still be very good, and if you run into others, they will be few. These are the days you can pick your place according to your mood and probably find no one else already parked when you arrive. Also, if you arrive early enough, you can stake out a space from which to work the evening hatches.

The signs of people been and gone are often, somehow, pretty in spite of themselves and their histories.

A Dunking, a Big Fish and Breakfast

There are a number of rivers on which I've caught more and bigger fish, but there are days and moments I've had here that I wouldn't trade for anything. There was the day when Mike Monson and I fished through the annular eclipse so intent on casting to the banks along a wide, flat stretch outside of Amherst, that we thought it was merely clouds passing and never looked up. Mike had a great laugh at my expense that day when I fell over in waist-deep water, soaking myself to the inside of my hat. He said he had never seen anyone take a fall quite like it. A couple hours later, when he took one step too

far without looking and went in over *his* head, I didn't crack a smile. When he sputtered back to his feet and looked at me sitting on the rocks nearby, after regaining his own hat, I simply mentioned how amazing it could be that a person could be upright and dry one moment, then prone and soaked the next. I assured him it could happen to anyone. Great fun. Grand total fish caught: One seven-inch brook trout.

A couple years ago, while scouting for places to take my mother-in-law for her first trout excursion ever, I had one of those days all to myself when everything clicked. It was magical. I arrived on the upper Tomorrow shortly after sunup and fished at a dozen different stops from there downstream before heading home in the early evening. At each stop, I caught at least one gorgeous little brook trout. I never saw a brown all day. The next day, my mother-in-law caught her first trout, a 12-inch brookie.

More recently, Dan Wendelborn and I fished the lower river on a golden day when the surface of the water reflected the trees with such a depth of color that the river was a perfect mirror image of the trees lining its banks: A river of gold and orange and yellow and red. A couple weeks later, I caught my biggest fish yet in one of the trophy sections of the river. I had heard stories, and I had seen pictures of large fish from the river just below Nelsonville, but had never caught anything there over eight, maybe nine inches myself. The fish I caught was no more a trophy than every fish is a trophy, but it was big enough and beautiful.

I have a vague memory of fishing the upper Tomorrow back in the '60s. It is a memory not entirely clear and therefore not completely trustworthy. What I remember is water not unlike all of the other brook trout streams in the area. I recall heavy brush at streamside, a great deal of deep, sticky muck, long branches overhanging the river and a frying pan with four cornmeal-coated brookies in a house that smelled like breakfast.

A few years ago, I came back to the Tomorrow after some years away, and the changes I saw made it look a much healthier and more productive river than the one of my youth. In the past few years, it has gotten even better. That place where I remember catching the brookies some 30 years ago still holds a nice population of the colorful little natives. The rest of the river down to Waupaca, however, now holds not only native brookies, but a good population of naturally reproducing wild browns. There's still some stocking of the Tomorrow (Waupaca), the difference is that most of the fish put in the river these days are from wild stock. And it can be expected that one day, if we do things right, this stream will be one of those that fulfills the Wisconsin dream of all clear, cold streams populated by wild trout.

What Tomorrow Trout Eat

Hatches on the Tomorrow are relatively consistent. Though, as mentioned earlier, this river really comes into its own in the evening and at night. During spring, you can expect to see a few black stoneflies and a growing population of blue-winged olives. Tan caddis will begin to appear around early May.

Above: Dan Wendelborn prospects a treacherous,
but productive, piece of the Tomorrow.
Right: Josh Halla awaits the strike on a narrow corridor.
Left: Blizzard fishing for big browns on the first day of
Wisconsin's early season.

Beginning in late May and early June, you can expect to see the first of the Sulphur emergences, along with a few black quills. While the Sulphur emergence may never be known as a super hatch, catch it on the right evening and you can have some good fun.

Between mid-June and mid-July, the Hex comes off. This is a time of sweet madness, not to be indulged in by the weak of heart or those afraid of the dark. The bugs are large, the fish are large, the fishers smell of cheap tobacco and all manner of home-brewed bug dope. The heartiest of these are normally sane people who will camp at streamside for two or three weeks at a time, fishing at night and sleeping during the day so they might fish another night. Usually their families know where they are and trust that they will return to their senses when the Hex hatch subsides.

A variety of caddisflies hatch during the length of the summer, sometimes in great numbers. But the next big hatch after the Hex is the white fly, or white mayfly. This hatch can be as sporadic as the Hex can be. Catch it just right, on the other hand, and it can be like fishing in a snow storm. In fact, depending on who you talk to, the white fly hatch is an even bigger deal than the Hex.

For flies on the Tomorrow, arm yourself with a good complement of Gold Ribbed Hare's Ears and traditional Pheasant Tails, as well as Prince Nymphs. A handful of Copper Bobs (originated by artist and guide Bob White) will stand you in good stead, as will an emerging caddis pattern or two. You

Chuck Richards makes a slow float over
edge-dwelling brookies on
the upper Tomorrow.
Left: The Red Mill, a popular
tourist stop on the
Crystal River.

Bait hides out where an imitation is expected.

first choice, but something with a more natural (more sparsely dressed) silhouette might also be in order, such as a severely underdressed White Wulff. And, naturally, you will want to have your favorite hopper and ant patterns on hand for those days when the breeze is sprinkling terrestrials on the water's surface.

What Tomorrow Fishers Eat

Speaking of food, Waupaca, Stevens Point and the little villages of the area offer a wide variety of table fare. My personal favorite in the area, for any meal and good companionship, is Stevens Point's Hilltop Bar & Grill, just west of the intersection of highways 10 and 51. For lunch, another good bet is the Crystal Cafe in Iola. The Crystal is a traditional mid-America eatery where the pies attract diners from all over the state. The classic Crystal Cafe lunch is a burger and fries with a chocolate malt, followed by a piece of cherry (or apple, or blackberry) pie. If you're looking for a big burger, try Little Norway in Scandinavia. You won't believe the Ole Burger until you've seen and eaten one (of course, for lighter appetites—but not much lighter—there's the Lena Burger). And they have Point beer on tap. At night, try the Wheelhouse (just outside of Waupaca) for a pizza, or the Oakwood Supper Club in town for the kind of meals that have made Wisconsin supper clubs legendary.

should also carry a mix of adult caddis imitations. Elk Hair and Little Black Caddis, to be sure, but perhaps also a couple of size 14 or 16 Gray Caddis. For the most fun during the Hex hatch, have a couple of big duns and a couple of spinners. For the white fly hatch, the White Wulff is a common (and good)

Still life with Tomorrow River rod built by Dave Bell.

Flume Creek

Counties: **Waupaca, Portage**
Nearest Communities: **Iola, Stevens Point**
Fly/Bait Shop, Guide Service: **One Stop Sport Shop**
(Stevens Point)

When I was about 14, my folks went looking for a place from which to make a home away from home, a place to which they would eventually retire. I lacked Mom and Dad's vision, their ability to see below the surface. So when they lit upon an old 40-acre homestead just inside the Portage County line in north central Wisconsin, all I could see was a 100-plus-year-old down-at-the-heels shack and a set of out-buildings with their better days beyond the sweep of memory. That is to say, its charms were lost on me.

The Shack, as we called it for years afterward, did however hold certain appeal even for the unappreciative and preoccupied teenager I was back then. It was 1963, and there was little room in my life for much besides girls, rock & roll and my buddies.

I saw and shot my first ruffed grouse on the logging trail below the Shack and later would limit out there regularly. The deer hunting was unbeatable. And, as Dad already knew when we first went to look at the place, the brook trout fishing in every direction was nothing less than phenomenal.

It was, I like to think from my current point-of-view, the trout that caused my parents to buy the Shack and repair it and groom three acres of lawn and plant over two acres of vegetable garden and put in flowers that came up everywhere you expected and least expected flowers to be and even install indoor plumbing and electricity for retirement when retirement came. These are the kinds of things hard-working folk might do to make a nice place for themselves in the country of trout. Mom and Dad were nothing if not hard-working.

I would like to be able to say that I explored all the streams near the Shack with my father, but the fact is, we didn't fish (or do anything else) much together: As noted earlier, I was too busy with less important things. Dad, however, came to know the area well. If he had a favorite piece of water, it must

Skinny Peterson Creek has yielded one or two outsized fish amongst its numerous small fry.

have been Flume Creek. The brookies were abundant through most of the stream, and below the millpond dam at Northland, he happily baited and re-baited hooks for my little nephew and niece as they landed panfish with delight and abandon.

In 1968, Dad took my new girlfriend and I to a favorite stretch of Flume Creek for a rare day on the stream together. On a summer day in 1975, less than a year after Dad died, I took my wife and Mom fishing on another stretch of Flume where there might be memories if not fish. After that, it would be almost 20 years before I fished Flume Creek again.

Life changes and the need to find true home water for myself brought me back to the trout streams of Waupaca and Portage counties a couple years ago. It took almost no time at all for the appeal of Flume Creek to win me over. Surprisingly, much of the creek was just as I remembered it. Some of it had changed, but where change had come, it was for the better.

My favorite place to fish Flume Creek these days is at, and upstream from, Northland. With the blessing and cooperation of Waupaca County, the dam at Northland was removed in 1994. The old millpond was over 100 years old and serving no useful purpose. Stream improvement work, funded by trout stamp money, was done in 1996 by a DNR habitat crew. The result is a beautiful stretch of trout water that winds through meadow and into woods. There, a stealthy fisher might come upon a deep-shaded hole where some of Flume Creek's larger fish hold court on the inside of a bend. It isn't easy to cast here, but a well-placed cast could score a strike. It's the kind of hole where you only get one chance due to the disruptive nature of a large trout hooked in a small space.

Note that when the term "large" is used to describe Flume Creek trout, it is relative. Brookies from four to nine inches are typical; over ten inches relatively rare. It's hard to say how big the browns get. According to a local fellow I talked to on my last trip, a recent DNR shocking turned up not a trout over twelve inches. My own first fish out of Flume this year was a dark thirteen-inch brown. I have seen bigger.

Downstream from Highway 49 at Northland, the greenery can be heavy. But there are plenty of fish, some of them holding in very deep water. During our early trout season in March this year I had great fun working a patiently holding pod of uncharacteristically large brookies with one of Rich Osthoff's big black and grizzly Bi-Buggers.

West (upstream) from Northland, there are several other access points. At one, you go down from the road, into the woods and pick your way along, fishing the fly-fishable stretches. At another, you hike through a tall grass field and work back upstream to the road, with casting easy *most* of the way.

Flume Creek's bottom offers as much variety as its surroundings. Here, the bottom is gravel. There, it's sand. Over there, it's peppered with large rocks left by the last glacier. Wading is often easy, though rocky areas in particular can be tricky.

In Waupaca County, there are four and a half miles of Class I trout stream and three miles of Class II. In Portage County, the DNR lists almost seven miles of Class I water and

Some places, some days, a good pair of waterproof boots is enough.

over four of Class II. That totals to about eighteen miles of stream with a healthy population of naturally reproducing brookies and browns. Other than at Northland, fishing pressure is light. And even there you're seldom crowded. While Flume Creek has its devotees, other, better-known area streams attract the lion's share of the fishing traffic.

My experience suggests that great hatches are not a common occurrence on Flume Creek, though I might be wrong. I've seen only one truly heavy emergence, that being a size 16 tan caddis. Two of us caught fish during that two-hour bug show that were so full they seemed incapable of stuffing even one more bite into their mouths.

At other times, I've run into minor emergences of Sulphurs and blue-winged olives. Of course there are also the usual Midwestern encounters with tiny midges and Tricos for which I never seem to have just the right match.

If you carry a selection of size 14-18 Adams; Blue-Winged Olives in 16 and 18; Pheasant Tails and Hare's Ears in 12, 14 and 16; as well as a size 20 or 22 Griffith's Gnat, you'll be pretty well prepared for most days on Flume. Add a small hopper, an ant or two and a black and brown cricket for mid- to late summer fishing.

I've fished Flume with my wife, my son and several others, but I like the creek best when I fish it alone. Those are the times I can fish it with my father the way I wish I had when he was alive.

Is he really there with me now? I don't know for sure. I talk to him, but he never answers...out loud.

Little Wolf River

Counties: **Waupaca, Portage, Marathon**
Nearest Communities: **Waupaca, Iola, Big Falls**
Fly/Bait Shop, Guide Service: **One Stop Sport Shop**
(Stevens Point)

I could begin by telling you that trout fishers like the Little Wolf because it is, as every last one of them say, like a miniature Wolf River. Or because it is like a miniature of their favorite western freestoner. Or, I could begin by telling you it is beautiful. But I'd rather begin with a random set of images that pop to mind every time I head for the Little Wolf.

There is my mother-in-law on her first trout hunt. I've positioned her on the bank, below a bridge, on a wide stretch of river that is also deep. This is the tail end of Little Wolf trout water, but I'm told there can be some large fish here. She casts. Hooks up! I'm floored. So far on this long day she has caught one very nice brookie just a few miles back on Flume Creek. That's it. And now, on her first cast, she's into another fish. It fights large. She reels it in. I net the nicest Little Wolf perch I have ever seen. (It is also the only perch I have ever seen this far up on this river.)

On another day, I park at a marked DNR parking area (the only car there) and head in the direction I assume the river to be. There is no trail. After what seems to be a little too long a walk, I go back to the car—once I find the way—to check the

Summer in full foliage on the Little Wolf. Tie on a spider; or a Black Bivisible will do.

Gazetteer to see what the shape of the river is in this place. Fortified with this new knowledge, I find the river...eventually. It is gorgeous. It is a fly-fisher's dream. It is being mined by a couple of locals, each with a stringer of brookies trailing off his belt loop in the water behind and ultra-light spin tackle coupled to big wads of worms. I head downstream to fish below them and find their brothers engaged in the same sport.

An end-of-season outing finds my partner and me on a piece of river we haven't fished before. There is a cottage buried back in the trees, at the end of a long dirt two-track, across from the designated parking area. There are the remnants of an old bridge that makes one wonder what a bridge was doing back here anyway. The water is wide and easy to fish, except where willows hang across the river and make anything but ducking impossible. As I get to each tree, I go down as low as I am able without performing a do-it-yourself baptism and promptly stick my face in a thick, sticky spider web occupied by a large, hairy spider unmatched by anything in my fly box. I repeat this exact same experience several times on my march upstream. For the next week, I will dream of nothing but large, hairy spiders that guard every

A walking stick about to take an Adams.

Rare and fragile Indian pipe.

trout stream I wish to fish. (Later that day, I was rewarded with a big eddie occupied by several respectable browns that greedily swallowed my fly. I was fishing a size 8 Black Bivisible.)

The branches of the Little Wolf offer up over 30 stream miles through Marathon, Portage and Waupaca counties. Approximately five of that is Class I water split between the three counties. The other 25 miles is Class II. Browns and brookies can be found throughout the system. The brookies

are native. Some of the browns are wild in Marathon and Portage counties. To the best of my knowledge, most Waupaca County Little Wolf browns are planted.

To tell the truth, I'm always happy to catch browns—wild *or* planted—here, but I come to the Little Wolf hoping and expecting to catch the brook trout. My theory is that somewhere in this multi-branched river there resides large brookies. Why? Because I think I remember them from my youth, and because there's this dream I have sometimes. Scoff if you like, but I've heard a lot of theories even more lame than this one.

One thing I can tell you with certainty is that the Little Wolf and its feeders contain a phenomenal number of little brook trout. In some stretches, there are nothing but brookies ranging in size from three inches to four, maybe occasionally five. Magic might happen when one of these miniatures grows up to be a porker eating her brothers and sisters as well as the generous variety of insects available.

Access to the Little Wolf is good at bridge crossings and at a handful of marked DNR parking areas. To prospect the Little Wolf, travel Highway 49 and peek into the side roads that branch off to either side. As far as crowding, the Little Wolf only seems to get hit hard the first few days of the season. Usually you can take your pick of fishing spots and have them all to yourself. As a rule of thumb, the farther up you fish, the better the fishing will be. During the early and late season, however, don't be surprised if the tail end of the trout waters deliver some nice fish...including an occasional perch.

Plover River

Counties: Portage, Marathon
Nearest Communities: Wausau, Stevens Point
Fly/Bait Shop: Gander Mountain (Wausau)

I've been told there used to be very large trout in the Plover River, that in the early '90s they got fished out, that now they're returning. Any of it may be true. My own experience says there are many brookies, some of them big enough to take care of themselves, and a fine sampling of wild browns from 12 to 14 inches. I have never seen a brown in the 20-inch range in the Plover, nor have I seen a 16-inch brookie, but rumors are that there are a few. It would please me to believe this to be true. (It would please me even more to see one.)

Experience also tells me that there are many chubs in the lower river that have fooled more than one wishful thinker into believing they are trout on the first few missed takes. Ditto some outsized suckers. If trout eat chubs, they don't eat enough of them. And the suckers are just too damn big (and ugly) for anything to eat. Besides, in addition to healthy bug populations, there is enough meat (in the form of crayfish and little fishes) living in the Plover for the trout to be fairly selective.

Essentials

The Plover begins in swamp and cold-water springs just above the Langlade County line then flows roughly 25 miles from the top of Marathon County toward the bottom on the county's east side. The river doesn't end here, but the trout, for the most part, do. The nine miles between the headwaters and County Highway N are designated Class I water with native brookies and naturally reproducing browns. From CTH N down to Highway 153 at the village of Bevent is Class II, with some of the same browns and brooks, as well as planted browns and rainbows.

Access on the river is excellent with more than a dozen bridge crossings and designated public parking areas. Once

Tom Magnuson draws a perfect loop (for the prevailing conditions) over a narrow lane.

you are in the river—opportunities for angling from shore are limited—you'll find a bottom that varies from gravel to sand to muck. On my wife's very first visit to the Plover, she found herself above the thighs—and sinking—in deep, sucking muck at river's edge. I can, even now, hear her nervous calls for help as I tried to land an ill-tempered brown 75 feet downstream of her. (She still complains that I landed the fish before coming to her aid. I had once stepped in the same hole she was in myself and knew she wouldn't sink much deeper. She is a stubborn woman and refuses to take comfort in this fact.)

As long as you stay out of the muck and steer wide of the deepest holes, the Plover is mostly an easy wade. Simply observe the same basic rules of wading you would anywhere: Look the water over before you step in; take every step with care; never underestimate a river or overestimate yourself.

On much of the Plover, casting is a breeze. This is a woodland Wisconsin stream, however, and there are places where casting *is* difficult, others where only a perfect roll cast will work, and a few where dapping must be the method of choice if you are to fish at all.

Favorite Places

While not beautiful in the sense the Little Wolf is, the Plover is pretty here and handsome there. I have a couple of favorite places.

One is above and below the CTH N bridge, in Marathon County, where I have seen some of the best evening spinner falls of anywhere in Wisconsin. The water is wide, casting

*Left: Kathy Magnuson and
Janet Halla shop for the fly of the day.
Below: A miracle of yellow and orange near river's edge.*

easy. It's one of those places that fools you. Casting *is* easy, but casting *well* is tricky. The cast has to be subtle and unseen by the fish. Your fly has to hit the surface just right in just the right place, then drift free of any hint of drag over the waiting trout that smile up in derision. I have fished here alone on a quiet evening, and I'm sure I heard name calling and ridicule directed at me from below the surface. These fish may not be smarter than I am, but they are instinctually superior. *Sometimes* one of them lets me catch her. The latter reminds me of the pretty girl who let's you kiss her once so you know to your soul how much it can hurt to never kiss her again.

My other favorite place on the Plover is the Special Regulations section from CTH Z up. There have been great nymph days here, great dry-fly days and a few days when I had to pretend I didn't care if I caught fish or not. The latter isn't that difficult when you're on a narrow, winding strip of clear, clean black water, bordered by green and a white puff cloud and blue sky. It is a place to be and feel alone; alone with the birds and the fishes. And if there are huge brook trout in the Plover, this is where I think they might be.

What to Fish With

As on most Wisconsin streams, my own preferred approach is upstream or up-and-across, but there are some nice wide pieces of water here where down-and-across can be very effective. Anywhere you see a big rock, you will want to cast both in front and in back of it, no matter which direction you're fishing.

Take the time to try to see what the trout are up to before you begin fishing. A few minutes' wait, spent in productive observation could be the difference between seeing or missing a subtle morning emergence or a light spinner fall at dusk. You have to watch. You have to know what the fish are taking, if they are visibly taking anything. It might be a summer evening rise of little yellow sallies or a daytime emergence of tan caddis. I've seen some truly subtle Sulphur hatches and had sporadic, cloudy-day encounters with blue-winged olives. If you are very lucky, you may hit a big brown drake hatch or fall in June, or a Hex hatch over those muck bottoms from a couple of weeks to a month later.

In general, no-hackle imitations of whatever's coming off are a good choice. One exception I can't explain is the Brown Bivisible which seems sometimes to be just the thing for this water and these fish. Below the surface, Pheasant Tails, Gold Ribbed Hare's Ears and Prince Nymphs work as well on the Plover as anywhere. For streamers, try either a Little Brown Trout, Little Brook Trout or a Black Nose Dace. And if you want to try a meat imitation, go with a small, dark Crayfish.

Whatever you fish with, wherever you fish, take your time. Let the river pace both your step and your cast. Each river has its own rhythm, its own tempo. The Plover is a waltz.

One of those places where
only the longest leader and the finest tippet will suffice.

Central

Mecan River

Counties: **Waushara, Marquette**
Nearest Communities: **Wautoma, Montello, Wild Rose**
Fly/Bait Shop, Guide Service: **Wild Rose Fly Shop**
   (Wild Rose)

If you don't live in Wisconsin or one of our neighboring states, chances are you haven't heard of Waushara County. The Mecan, White, Pine and Willow rivers, Chaffee and Wedde creeks, Pearl Lake and the Wild Rose Mill Pond may not ring even a single bell. On the other hand, it *is* possible, in the course of conversation with fishers who know this country or who have visited, that you have heard stories about legendary Hex hatches, mosquitoes that can drain a man of blood in minutes, and his dog in half that time. It's possible that you heard somewhere, a few years back, about a dead hippopotamus at midstream (I'll explain soon).

Waushara County has over 30 trout streams and some 100 lakes and ponds. Pretty much any direction you turn, there's a place to fish. And a great deal of it is fly-fishable. This is a glitz-free tourist haven; a county marked by commercial campgrounds and noncommercial retreats, supper clubs, sand beaches and sunburns. (File away in the back of your mind right now that all of these tourists are likely to be the reason locals value their "private property" so highly and won't be bashful about letting you know it if you should wander onto their posted *or unposted* land.)

My Dad told me years ago how the brush was so thick you had to crawl on your belly to get to many of the best Waushara County trout streams and how, once there, you had to fish from your knees, because there wasn't room to stand up. He also fished the County's still water. As a kid, I was seldom allowed to go along on the Saturday night fishing excursions to Pearl Lake that Dad made with buddies like Earl Zelmer, but I saw the huge trout in the sink on Sunday morning, and was filled with amazement.

The one time I do recall going along, I sat between Mom and Dad in the rented green, wooden row boat. A Coleman lantern hung over one side, we fished from the other. The air was thick with mosquitoes and the ineffective smoke of Camel cigarettes. Guy Mitchell, Theresa Brewer and Buddy Knox brought rhythm to the dark. The fish bit all night long. I think it must have been wonderful.

Given my preference for trout in moving water, I don't fish Waushara still water with any regularity, though I'm told it's still excellent. If you are in the vicinity and you want to fish well-known still water, consider Green Lake. It's big, it's deep, it's cold and it's loaded with fish. In fact, it holds so many of Wisconsin's favorite fish (including trout) that it's sort of like an aquarium on which you can launch a boat.

These days I go to Waushara County as often as not when

A new Wisconsin covered bridge with trout both up and down.

I'm not sure what I want, when I'm just looking for a place to fish. And while many Waushara County faithful have their favorite stream that they always go to first, I go strictly on the mood of the day.

Perhaps the Waushara stream I fish most often is the Mecan River, and I've taken a fair number of fish there. Yet my favorite Mecan memories have few fish in them. What sticks better in the mind are days like the one Janet looked up to see what was "buzzing" in the tree branches just over her head and was startled to see a "swarm" of hummingbirds within arm's reach. Or the day my nephew Erik inquired loudly of me downstream whether the area's snakes were poisonous, and should he be concerned about the large black one swimming toward him?

Everyone who knows the story likes to tell those who don't about the hippopotamus that greeted wading fishers on Opening Day of 1994. The hippo was dead, but even a dead hippo is quite a surprise on a central Wisconsin trout stream. The beast had wandered from its zoo-farm home and expired in the middle of the river. I don't recall anymore whether the hippo was dispatched by its owner or died of natural causes. On the other hand, I guess when you consider the circumstances, the word *natural* does seem out of place.

The Mecan offers up about 10 miles of Class I and II water in Waushara County with another six miles or so in Marquette County. My experience here is mostly with browns, but there have been some rainbows, and a few brookies. According to the DNR, all naturally reproduce here.

Avid Hex-hatch followers have a special place in their hearts for the Mecan. The wide, flat stretches of sand-bottomed stream, edged in muck are considered by some to offer the best Hex fishing in the Badger state. When it is good, it can be phenomenal. The bugs are huge, and on the two or three best nights, clouds of them emerge to the gulp and splash of trout larger than you might expect to find in such a stream. Most of us will offer up a couple of sleepless nights on the hope of hitting the hatch just right. The guys who have the best of it, however, are those who abandon jobs, families and hope of ever regaining their sanity (to say nothing of their once-human scent) for the chance of a perfect night of casting in the dark to big invisible trout. The rest of us openly admire their dedication, their madness, their perhaps lost souls.

My own best Hex story comes from another Waushara County stream, the White River, but it could as easily have taken place on the nearby Mecan. I talked Mike Monson into leaving his new bride for the evening and accompanying me on the search for giant mayflies and trout to match. He showed minor concern about fishing in the dark in a place where the muck and mud at streamside could suck you in and possibly swallow you whole if a buddy wasn't along to pull you out, but he agreed as how the prize seemed worth whatever risk might present itself.

We arrived at the river early in order to pick our spots while there was still light in the sky (and to get a jump on the other fishers who would be along presently). We scouted around a bit and made sure we knew the way back out of the stream well enough to navigate it when all light was gone. We started fishing before dark, because we had seen a few of the megabugs come off, and because we couldn't wait. We were ready. I don't know what Mike was fishing with, but I had on a great tan thing with white hair wings that looked like a prop from a '50s science fiction movie. Mike began casting. I watched the water. When fish began to rise, I threw my first cast across stream. In an explosion of sound and water, a brown bigger than any I had yet landed smashed my fly with such violence that Mike later described it as being like

A place where the water is skinny and the fish are spooky.

someone had thrown an anvil into the water between us. Mike stood watching, eyes wide, mouth agape, his own fly floating unnoticed downstream. I struggled with the spotted monster. My leader seemed about to snap, I let him have a little line. Mistake. He took me into a tangle across stream and broke me off. The line shot back with such velocity that, but for my glasses, I might have lost an eye. When I examined what was left of my leader, what I saw was what it might look like if the heavy end of the mono had contained a charge of black powder.

I replaced the leader and tied on another fly just like the one recently lost. As my second cast touched the surface, it was nailed. Mike was speechless. This fish was clearly not as large as the first, but it was large enough. This time I played it a bit smarter and brought it to net. It was a crappie big enough to hang over both sides of the frying pan. I was so disappointed it wasn't a trout, that I released it before I thought about what a fine breakfast it would have made. I won't repeat what Mike had to say about that: Suffice to say he was no longer speechless.

Other Waushara Streams

Another Waushara County stream I've spent some time around, but not fished much, or very successfully for that matter, is the Pine River. Dad used to fish it fairly often with some success. And a couple of fellows I know who don't lie any more than the average fisher told me of some magnificent days they've had there. Everything, including DNR reports, tells me this is a stream I need to put more time into. There's approximately 23 miles of Class I and II stream with naturally reproducing brook and brown trout.

The trout streams of Waushara County are generally fairly low flow, with their share of classic riffle-run-pool stretches. They average between 10 and maybe 30 feet in width. Bottoms range from heavy cobble to sand (this area has *a lot* of sand) to that deep muck certain mayflies and mosquitoes love so well. The surrounding environment varies from heavily wooded with thick brush to open pasture and meadow. On the hottest days of summer, when the wider shallow stretches of water run warm and beer clear, the trout hide under banks or move up into the deeper darker environs. This latter is a good time to try some of the county's skinny little creeks noted for their inhospitable attitude toward fly-fishers: Disagreeable though they may be, there are some jewels here.

How To Find It

The best way to begin planning a trip to Waushara County would be with a comparison between the Wisconsin trout regs book and either the DeLorme *Atlas & Gazetteer* or the Milwaukee Map Company map for this part of the state. The more detailed maps you use, the better. Think of highways 21, running east/west, and 51, running north/south, as your anchor points, then work out from them. There's plenty of public access to streams, but you do need to be careful not to stray onto private lands. The DNR has tried to do a good job of posting signage at boundaries. With their short staff and

limited budget, however, they can't do it all; so watch out for yourself.

Food, Lodging, Attractions

The nearest communities of size are Wild Rose, Wautoma, Redgranite and Montello. All have a variety of lodging and eateries. Visitors who like the atmosphere of a bed & breakfast will find plenty to choose from, along with the usual (though not overwhelming) selection of motels. When it comes to eats, stick with the supper clubs, cafes and taverns. I've had many good dining experiences in the area, but haven't eaten at any one place often enough to call it a favorite. (The burgers at Reggie's in Wautoma *are* awfully good, however.) Antique and craft shops are plentiful, as are a variety of non-fishing outdoor activities. If time allows, a stop at the Wild Rose Fish Hatchery can be fun. If you have a float tube, you might want to give it a try on the Wild Rose Mill Pond.

*In the right setting,
there is nothing common about the common milkweed.*

Willow Creek

County: **Waushara**
Nearest Communities: **Red Granite, Wautoma, Wild Rose**
Fly/Bait Shop, Guide Service: **Wild Rose Fly Shop** (Wild Rose)

During Wisconsin's early inland trout season, Willow Creek makes a fine brook trout hunting ground. Browns reproduce naturally here as well, but usually, if I go, I'm thinking specks.

On a typical May day not long ago, my partner and I went when another stream we planned on fishing just didn't feel right. When we stepped into Willow Creek, we had visions of a brace of spring green brookies in the pan that evening. The temperature was unseasonably warm, the wind gusty, our total catch was one of the brownest brown trout we've ever seen. His size and shape indicated that he might have been consuming a steady diet of crayfish, sculpin and other larger cuts of meat. Which is to say that a typical day on Willow Creek will generally mean that whatever you expect to happen will not...but anything else might.

Willow Creek can be productive all season. My favorite times are early spring and late fall. There are even times during these seasonal extremes when the big creek seems almost predictable. The right fly fished in the right way at the right place at the right time is virtually guaranteed to attract a hungry, mid-sized brookie with a playful attitude.

During summer, when the water warms, things are pretty much catch-as-catch-can—so to speak—but skill and patience can, and often do, win out. You may not see the brookies of the cooler seasons; they'll be hiding in deep, dark holes and skinny tributaries. Now, the browns will rule.

The 21 miles of Willow Creek trout water are divided roughly in half between Class I and Class II. As a rule of thumb, figure more brook trout in the upper reaches and more browns in the lower. Be prepared, however, for variations in water temperature to send all the trout scurrying (do trout scurry?) to one end or the other. On the warmest summer days, I'd say stay away altogether.

True to the nature of the stream, there seems to be no one fly that always works on Willow Creek. Blue-Winged Olives and Deer Hair Caddis in a variety of tonal variations come close over most of the fishing season. Hendricksons appear, to a degree, between mid-April and late May. Sulphurs can bring fish up in May and June. Find that right spot, and you can enjoy the Hex hatch here in late June and/or early July. During late summer and fall, terrestrials can be deadly. Hoppers make for exciting fishing. My favorites are good ol' Joe's and Dave's. Also try your favorite crickets, ants and beetles. Finding just the right pattern and color in the latter set can be difficult, but once found, the fish will sometimes be voracious.

Getting There

An easy approach to easy-access sections of the Willow can be had by taking Highway 21 west of Redgranite to CTH S north and pulling off at the "Willow Creek State Fishery" signs.

The Willow offers everything from slow and wide to fast and narrow.

Central

Lawrence Creek

County: **Marquette**
Nearest Communities: **Westfield, Pardeeville**

There are many trout fishers in Wisconsin who don't know where Lawrence Creek is, have never fished it, never even heard of it. And there are others who see it as perhaps the most important trout stream in the state. It has been called "perfect" and described as "a shrine." Speaking for myself, I can say that it *is* beautiful. And, if the religion is trout fishing, then certainly this is one of our churches.

For Craig Halla, summer burns
across the decision of which one from only a few.

There is no question that when you are chest deep in Lawrence Creek, you *are* worshipping in The Big Church.

It's narrow. There are places where, if you are standing in the middle of the stream and you stretch your arms and fingers out in opposite directions, you can touch both banks at once. I don't know if there's a single spot where it's over 12 feet wide (not including undercuts, that is). Although I've wondered more than once, as the cold spring water seeped over the top of my waders, if another few steps might not take me to a place where it is 12 feet deep.

It's clear and clean. Even in its deepest holes, you can see to the bottom (and, yes, it follows, the fish can see all the way to the top). According to those who know much more than I about such things, Lawrence Creek also appears to be as close to pollution free as you can get.

It's full of fish. The only trout here are wild brook trout. There are many of them. They don't get very big, averaging between six and eight inches, but they are a wonder to see, catch and hold. Due to the clarity of the water and perhaps the fishing pressure of years past, they are not as easy to catch as brook trout often can be.

What makes Lawrence Creek so special to its devotees, however, is no more the stream as it is today than it is the history which made it that stream. During the Fifties and Sixties, extensive research was carried out during and following a phenomenal amount of stream improvement work. Former fisheries biologist, and author of *Trout Stream Therapy*, Bob Hunt, was responsible, along with Oscar Brynildson and Ray White, for much of the research and streamwork on Lawrence Creek. In a technical bulletin authored for the WDNR in 1988, he says: "This long-term research project is the most thorough evaluation of trout habitat development done in Wisconsin. Approximately 38,000 board feet of lumber and 6,000 tons of rock were used to construct 86 pairs of bank covers and current deflectors... These structures helped to reduce surface area by 51%, increase average depth by 65%, increase pool area nearly 300% and increase underbank hiding cover more than 400%." All this in only one year, 1964, and on 3.3 miles of trout-stream! It is possible that no other example of "trout-stream therapy" has had as much affect and influence on habitat improvement in Wisconsin as the Lawrence Creek project.

With its marshy surroundings, Lawrence Creek is rich in both streamside and instream vegetation, which in turn makes it rich in fish food. Small nymphs and streamers can be very effective. And there are some good mayfly hatches so, while tricky, dry-fly and emerger fishing can be excellent as well. Sulphurs and *tiny* blue-winged olives can work well; the Sulphurs on brighter days, olives when it's overcast. Or you could just show up with a box full of little Adams in a variety of body colors. All the streamside grasses also make terrestrial fishing a good possibility.

Lawrence Creek may be one of those streams that a lot of folks won't go very far to fish, but anyone who gets close and doesn't make a stop is missing a fine experience and, perhaps, a spiritual moment.

Finding Your Way

To locate Lawrence Creek, take CTH E west of Westfield where Highway 51 brushes across the city's eastern edge. From there, follow Eagle Avenue further west to a couple of well-marked pull-offs.

Lawrence Creek is consistently narrow, deep, cold and very difficult.

Southeast
Milwaukee Area Streams

Counties: **Milwaukee, Racine**
Nearest Communities: **Racine, Kenosha, Milwaukee, Chicago**
Fly/Bait Shop, Guide Service: **DIY Rod & Tackle** (Racine)**; Fly Rod & Tackle** (Racine)**; Laake & Joys** (Milwaukee)

I f you are in the last place on earth you would have expected to catch a trout (or salmon), and you can smell *city*, you are standing at river's edge, and each of the fishers on either side of you are within touching distance and somehow everyone present seems pretty much okay with the situation, chances are that you are on the Root River. The *Milwaukee Journal*, as well as every Great Lakes steelhead and salmon web site, a couple of magazines, at least five radio stations, three or four TV channels and a handful of cults have made it known that *the fish are in the river.* The Root River, that is.

Most trout fishing in Wisconsin can be done with some semblance of solitude. That is rarely, if ever, the case on the Root. How crowded can it get? A friend who puts in more hours than the rest of us on Wisconsin's lower east coast swears that several times he has seen the same fish hooked by two anglers at once. As with the Kewaunee River, this is a major brood stream and a major site of return for lake-run trout and salmon. On a slow weekday, you might have a few feet of water to yourself. Skip weekends during peak runs.

Come early morning or midday at midweek.

In the course of the short six miles of stream where you can expect to find fish—between the Racine Harbor and Horlick Dam upstream—the Root varies considerably in width and depth, with a number of deep holes, runs and riffles. Flow is moderate as a rule, but as with most east coast Wisconsin streams, from the northern tip to the Illinois border, *all* things depend upon rainfall. The simple formula: No rain = no water = no fish.

The Root hosts steelhead runs across the calendar; spring, summer, fall and winter. There is also a fall run of coho and chinook salmon, and browns. This isn't to say that there are always trout or salmon of some sort in the river, but, given the right set of environmental circumstances, it *is* possible. (Best bet, if you will be traveling any distance, would be to check the Lake Michigan steelhead web sites or call one of the local bait shops.)

As might be expected, there is a great deal of development along the Root River. There are also, however, some nice

Nothing quite compares with the turbulence of a salmon in shallow water.

65

urban parks and a few pleasant, quieter spots. Dam areas attract the largest crowds of anglers on this and other east coast streams, which means that sometimes those areas most attractive to fly-fishers will be less crowded.

What and How

Your basic equipment list will include a six- to nine-weight rod tied to a floating line, terminating at a six- to nine-foot leader with two to four feet of 0X or 3X tippet. The fly attached to the tip of that tippet will, likely as not, be a basic egg pattern in bright orange, red, pink, chartreuse (go figure) or a combination of the above. Yes, it's a lot like bait-fishing, especially after you attach the correct weight split shot a foot or two above the fly, but the point *is* to catch fish, right?

Other tried-and-true fly patterns include Woolly Buggers, a variety of Maribou Leeches and Deceivers. All of

Troy Wise releases one of several steelhead taken on an unseasonably warm November day.

the above should be tied on size 4-8 hooks. The egg colors listed above could all work here too, as could purple, black or crimson. Woolly Buggers, in particular, will benefit from the addition of some synthetic sparkle or flash. Salmon Candy, a conehead pattern developed by local fly-fisher, Troy Wise, has also been known to take a few fish on the right day.

Much, if not most of your casting will be done from shore or very shallow water. But you need to dress for the possibility of immersion and crashing, caroming pursuits along stream edges to maintain even the most tenuous hold on hooked salmonids. Should you end up in the water, you will want to be prepared for what could be a bone-chilling experience if you are improperly dressed. Except during the warmest summer-run days, think long underwear, sock liners and either neoprene or breathable materials over fleece. Dress to shed a few layers if necessary, but don't underestimate the potentially severe effects of spring and fall water temperatures.

The method of casting most commonly employed by steelhead and salmon fishermen (because they have no choice) is one described in less than poetic terms as "chuck and duck." Once one attaches an awkwardly constructed lure to a short, heavy leader and weights it with a substantial mass of lead or lead-like substance, the concept of casting gracefully pretty much falls by the way. This approach may not replicate the beautiful rhythms of dry-fly fishing, but

skilled practitioners can and do hook and land their share of fish. (And, yes, some of them do pierce their own ears free of charge in the process.)

Among the most successful fishers, opinions vary as to best approach (surprise, surprise). One method that seems very effective is to cast above holding females—or the place you expect them to be—and drift your fly, just above bottom, into the mouths of waiting males downstream. You want to get the fly deep quickly so it bounces up off the redd to its target, ideally without disturbing females setting on redds. While it may be awkward, precision casting is a must, and relatively drag-free drifts are helpful if not essential.

If the above doesn't work, try quartering upstream, immediately followed by a big upstream mend, then allowing your fly to drift down and swing. Slack must be avoided completely so that you can feel the "tick, tick, tick" when a fishstrikes. Strike indicators (bobbers: "a rose by any other name...") may be helpful until you develop a "feel" for this kind of fishing.

Additional Opportunities

While the Root River is perhaps the best- known stream of the southeast coast, it does have neighbors that offer the same set of opportunities, often without as much competition for space. Excellent examples would be Oak Creek, the Menomonee and Milwaukee rivers.

The Milwaukee River in Kletzsch Park.

Oak Creek, in the town of Oak Creek, offers anglers the opportunity to fish for the biggest migratory trout and salmon in a small-stream setting and sometimes without the people pressures common to the Root River. Here there are riffles, runs and pools, sometimes in a woodland setting. A stream bottom that includes everything from sand and gravel, to cobble, to boulders, to a Lannon Stone inlay, has proven very inviting to the anadromous fishes.

If there are Wisconsin trout streams that define "urban angling," they are the Menomonee and Milwaukee. On one hand, these waters seem so contradictory to their larger setting that they are hard to imagine. On the other hand, they fit as naturally as grass and trees into Milwaukee's superb parks environment. A single visit to either Kletzsch or Estabrook Park on the right day will quickly win you over.

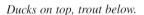

Ducks on top, trout below.

The Route To Big-Trout City

The Root is easily located by taking Racine County Highway K East off of Interstate 94 to State 38. Along 38, you will see an obvious pull-off or two, but good angling can also be had at Lincoln Park, immediately west of 38 in the city of Racine.

Estabrook Park is very near downtown Milwaukee. To find it, take 43 to Capitol Drive east. The park road is on the north side of the street, just after you cross the Milwaukee River. Kletzsch Park, not far away, is east off Green Bay Road, north of Silver Spring Drive. Both Estabrook and Kletzsch are examples of Milwaukee's fine parks system.

Black Earth Creek

County: **Dane**
Nearest Communities: **Madison, Cross Plains, Black Earth**
Fly/Bait Shop, Guide Service: **Fontana Sports Specialties** (Madison)**; Lunde's Fly Fishing Chalet** (Mt. Horeb)**; Madison Outfitters** (Madison)**; Steve Gerhardt Sporting Goods** (Madison)

S eptember 30. It is the last day of the inland trout season. It is noon, and it is raining a steady gray rain that shows no sign of letting up before day's end. The spaces between the hills are lined with fog that looks like smoke rising. For an instant, I am reminded of the Blue Ridge.

Fall color is making its crimson-orange-yellow-lime-green-gray-brown-purple crawl across Wisconsin, but, for the most part, it hasn't yet arrived in full dress along the banks of Black Earth Creek where I am setting in my car in my waders, unsure if I'll be fishing anymore today or not. I am waiting for signs of light along the dark green tree edges in the distance.

I am set on casting the last fly of the season onto Black Earth Creek: Forget for now the streams that dump into Michigan and Superior with their steelhead, salmon and brown trout runs; forget the extended seasons on the Peshtigo and the Wolf; this is the last day of the regular, inland trout season, and I intend to end it here. I'm thinking I might even catch a big trout today; something I don't do very often on Black Earth Creek.

The Color of a Stream

Black Earth Creek is a trout stream with many big-fish stories, but none of them are mine. I keep coming back, because I know the fish are here, and one day I will learn how to catch them. For most fishers, Black Earth is a stream that must be learned. Only a few—damn few—come here and fish it well on their first pass.

A few years back, Ron Manz, who many Midwesterners know as a master guide on the Bois Brule, was telling me about his luck on Black Earth one evening fishing his Ostrich Herl Leech. Seems he was fishing with a couple of the local know-it-alls who told him how difficult the big Black Earth trout were to lure out of their lairs. Thing was, while the locals were talking, Ron was catching those very same fish. He laid *all* the credit to the Ostrich Herl Leech (of his own design, and it's a good one), but there is something to be said, I think, for the nearly magical abilities of some fly-fishers. (There are folks who can calm crying babies, others who whisper to horses and a rare few who can catch trout anywhere.)

The author fishes at a favorite resting spot on Black Earth Creek.

In Wisconsin we've all heard and read numerous stories of the large and plentiful trout of Black Earth. I assume them (most of them anyway) to be true. I know fishers have a reputation for playing fast and loose with the truth, but with the exception of those standard trout stream encounters where we expect, even encourage, each other to take creative license with the facts, trout-fishers in general strike me as a relatively honest group. Besides, the evidence is overwhelming. A number of 20-plus-inch browns have been caught (and recorded) and shocked out of Black Earth. There is also no question that some stretches of the stream hold nearly phenomenal numbers of trout over 12 inches. This is a great stream, and a healthy one. It holds numerous trout (the DNR reports 1600 per mile), some of them quite large. It's just that a few of us have had more luck (skill) catching them than others.

Black Earth Creek begins with cold-water spring eruptions in the wetland just west of Wisconsin's capital city of Madison and wiggles its way across the edge of the driftless area until it empties into the Wisconsin River. Roughly 12 miles of trout holding water have caused it to be named one of America's 100 best trout streams by *Trout* magazine and to become the darling of a large population of local fly-fishers, as well as numerous visitors from Illinois, Iowa, Minnesota and, of course, elsewhere in Wisconsin. It is common, even on a weekday, to encounter license plates from all four states in your search for a place to fish. In fact, I have never been to Black Earth Creek on a day during the fishing season when there weren't at least two or three other fishers out before I got there.

Most of Black Earth Creek is easy to wade, although there are a number of spots where you would be better advised to get down on your knees and cast from streamside (remembering, of course, to keep your backcast high to prevent it from "tying up" in the tall weeds and grasses behind you). The creek bottom is largely gravel and cobble with a few big rocks. And there are those stretches of deep, sucking muck ("silt" is too nice a word for this stuff) that makes for great Hex hatches in June and July.

How and What

While good casting technique, especially when combined with tiny flies and fine tippets, appears to be the quickest route to success on Black Earth Creek, it is also worth noting that this is one Wisconsin spring creek where there is often plenty

of room even for novices to improve their skills. In their fine book, *Exploring Wisconsin Trout Streams*, Born, Mayers, Morton and Sonzogni address the need for a delicate presentation: "It is a place where anglers often must resort to a #22

Black Earth Creek is one of the few places you will encounter wild rainbows in Wisconsin.

fly on a 7X tippet in order to claim success. Sometimes even that doesn't work on this temperamental stream. And the angler may feel privileged to survive a silt-slogging night-fishing trip, having snared what we jokingly call the 'Black Earth Creek Grand Slam'—a bat, a muskrat, a red-winged blackbird, and a chub, or the rough fish of your choice...." And these are guys who know the creek as well as anyone.

The most common trout in the stream (if any trout may be called common) are naturally reproducing browns, but many anglers also find themselves catching planted rainbows. There is even supposition that Black Earth Creek may be seeing limited natural rainbow reproduction. And there are a few reintroduced wild brookies. Water temperatures seldom rise above 70, and are often considerably cooler than that. There have been a number of very warm summer days when I thought I would wade wet and was sent back to the car for proper clothing by surprisingly chilly water. Only when water is low and flows slow are temperatures too high for even the brookies that find their way into Black Earth.

The Bugs, Etc...

In addition to good water temperatures, there is a variety of instream and streamside vegetation to provide hiding places for the trout and support a healthy food supply. Besides occasionally outstanding Hex hatches, Hendricksons come off between mid-April and mid-June, light Cahills from mid-June to early August and blue-winged olives from the first hint of warmth in the air to well after the end of the season. Little black caddis appear early in the season and peter out by sometime in June. Olive and tan caddis may be most plentiful during the first half of the season, but a size 14–18 Elk or Deer Hair Caddis will take fish all season.

Black Earth regulars have also reported stoneflies in late March and April, red quills in May, white mayflies on August evenings and midges as regularly as blue-winged olives. There is also a very healthy mosquito population which the trout don't seem interested in; perhaps because they keep some of the human population at bay.

Terrestrials are available from early spring through fall. While you're waiting for the hoppers and crickets to show up, you might choose a variety of ants, beetles and spiders as lures. For underwater prospecting, a good selection would include Hare's Ears, Pheasant Tails and Prince Nymphs, as well as scuds, leeches and Sow Bugs. One relatively reliable source tells us you can't beat a small Deer Hair Mouse for big nighttime browns.

Black Earth Creek is a stream rich in opportunity, if you're willing to take the time to learn it. I've put in more time trying to

Salmo Pond offers everyone the opportunity to catch trout, some of them as long as your leg.

On Black Earth, Den Halla learns that casts may need to be long; and perfect doesn't hurt either.

find success on this stream than I have on others, but I'm willing to put in more. When success does come, and I am catching big Black Earth trout with regularity, there is no question that the extended learning process will have been worth it.

Food & Lodging

One of the things Black Earth Creek has going for it that many trout streams do not is its proximity to a true wealth of good-to-great food and lodging. The small towns of the river and hill country west of Madison offer many motels, B&Bs and campgrounds, as well as a decent selection of supper clubs, cafes and taverns. Madison is so close that anyone seeking the ultimate in variety in lodging, food, drink, music and just about anything else that might come to mind is likely to find it there. (My personal vote for favorite Madison restaurant comes out a tie between Quivey's Grove just out of town and Porta Bella downtown. About a dozen other places around town tie for second.)

As well as being a great place to eat and sleep, the Black Earth Creek area and Madison cater well to the needs of fly-fishers and other outdoor folk. There are several excellent fly-shops, guides and outfitters, including Lunde's Fly Fishing Chalet south of Mt. Horeb. In Madison, you'll find Madison Outfitters, Fontana Sports Specialties and Steve Gerherdt's Sports.

Oh yeah, just in case you were wondering, that last day of the season ended on a high note. The sky cleared. The sun came out. The temperature rose. It was a beautiful afternoon and evening. I didn't break any bones, and I didn't drown.

Mount Vernon Creek

County: Dane

Nearest Communities: Mt. Vernon, Mt. Horeb, Verona, Madison

Fly/Bait Shop, Guide Service: **Fontana Sports Specialties** (Madison)**; Lunde's Fly Fishing Chalet** (Mt. Horeb)**; Madison Outfitters** (Madison)**; Steve Gerhardt Sporting Goods** (Madison)

My own experience notwithstanding, there are people who know these things better than I do who believe Mount Vernon Creek is more difficult to fish and find success on than Black Earth Creek a few miles up the road. Certainly, Mount Vernon often poses greater technical challenges to the fisher, and little of it offers the neophyte much hope. In terms of sheer numbers of fish caught by the author, however, I've done considerably better on Mount Vernon than on Black Earth. On Mount Vernon, fish were brought to hand on my first outing. It took a year before I caught anything more than a chill on Black Earth. It should probably also be noted that I haven't caught the really big fish that are known to be present on either stream.

Vitals

Mount Vernon Creek is eight miles long. In the DNR's old *Wisconsin Trout Streams* book, that eight miles is divided equally between Class I and Class II water. At this time, it would probably be fair to guess that more like two-thirds of the stream is now Class I. The same publication also shows that brook trout, brown trout and rainbows are all naturally reproducing in Mount Vernon. I don't recall ever taking a brookie or rainbow here, although brookies do live and breed in Mount Vernon feeders. The point is, when fishing this stream, expect—if you catch anything—to catch browns.

Finding a place to park along Mount Vernon Creek is easy with both designated public parking and well-worn pull-offs at road crossings. (On weekends, you can expect to find many, if not most, of these spaces occupied, however.) Fishing is not so simple. As noted earlier, Mount Vernon can be very challenging technically; as well as physically.

How to Catch a Fish

Early in the season, before instream and along-the-stream vegetation reaches its full glory, casting may be less difficult, but you will be more visible. By the time summer is up and running, grasses at streamside have moved from being the minor annoyance they occasionally were in early May to making the cast of a fly impossible or nearly so. And even though you will be better hidden (as long as you stay out of the stream), the trout are as spooky as ever; perhaps more so. All trout have lateral lines: Those in Mount Vernon Creek may also have ears, super-sensitive ears. We won't even discuss their ability to see through solid objects and around corners, for this is a

trait common to larger spring-creek trout throughout the southwestern part of the state. (That's how they got larger.)

As far as how to fish and what to fish with, the best advice may simply be to go light and be as non-invasive as possible. Both, I know, are pretty much basic advice for fishing this sort of stream. Here, however, carry the advice to its extreme. If you know a way to make yourself invisible, do it.

Fish a lightweight rod strung with lightweight line. Speaking of light, if your line is light gray in color, or light green, or possibly even light blue, or clear you will be much less likely to spook fish than with some of the high-visibility lines. Those latter have no place on Mount Vernon. Your tippet should probably be long, ending in either 6X or 7X.

If you can't identify a real insect to match with your fly, start small and dark. You may also want to use either no-hackle or sparsely hackled flies. Your casts will not have to be perfect as long as they appear so to the fish. How can you tell if your cast is good enough? Simply count the number of trout that use your fly to pierce their lip and divide by zero.

Bugs and meat available on Mount Vernon Creek will be a pretty close match to Black Earth Creek. The one outstanding exception may be that you will not find the prolific Hex hatch on Mount Vernon that you will on Black Earth. To tell you the truth, however, Mount Vernon would not be my first choice for night-fishing anyway.

If I was to offer one piece of advice for fishing Mount Vernon Creek, it would be don't be intimidated. If you happen to be in the early stages of developing your fly-fishing skills, either wait until you've progressed a bit to come here, or come early in the season when vegetation is less of a factor. On the other hand, if you have spent some time, as Jim Harrison says, "standing in a river waving a stick," have at it. Just stay low, look, listen, think before you cast, and then, cast perfectly with the perfect fly.

Finding Your Way

Take Highway 92 from Mt. Horeb to and through Mt. Vernon where it parallels the river. Where 92 meets County A, a triangle of a kind is created, through the center of which runs Mt. Vernon Creek.

Not Too Far From Here

It sometimes seems once you go west of Madison in the southern half of Wisconsin that every stream is a trout stream;

...happens even when I'm on my way to someplace else. And such a stream is Trout Creek.

Trout Creek is a stream with a great reputation and a proud history. There are those days when it's easy to see why and others when you have to shake your head and wonder why. On the good days, it's eight miles of Class I and II Iowa County trout stream populated by finicky wild browns. Forget the bad days.

When you reach Trout Creek, you have entered hilly, green country that feels right in all your senses. You are a little north of Barneveld, flattened by a tornado one day and rebuilt in a beer commercial another. You are a little south of Spring Green where Frank Lloyd Wright developed and made home to his architectural genius.

Trout Creek lies in a box created by Highways 18 and 151 to the south, 14 to the north, 78 to the east and 23 to the west. Given that, it's amazing how far you seem from anything but farm country two-lanes when you're there. My suggestion would be that if you are near-by, you should give it a try. You might hit one of the good days.

Trout Creek is small and challenging, but it is capable of yielding a surprise or two.

Southwest: Mount Vernon Creek

Big Green River

County: Grant

Nearest Communities: Fennimore, Boscobel, Prairie du
   Chien

Fishing Shop, Indian Summer Trout Co. Sport Shop
(Prairie du Chien)

When you go to fish the Big Green River, you will quickly find that it is closely tied to two other occasionally superb nearby trout streams—the Blue River and Castle Rock Creek. All three are found in Grant County at the Badger's extreme southwest corner. It's the kind of place where anyone you talk to who is fishing one is fishing the others. The Big Green is the major attraction of the three, so it is most likely to be mentioned first. For fishers new to Grant County, the Big Green is usually mentioned first due to a common newcomer's belief that the Blue and Castle Rock are secrets. This is also true of Grant County regulars who have caught one or two big brood stock plants on Castle Rock and think everyone else hasn't already heard about these 25- to 30-inch monsters. You will find, while looking for a pull-off on any nice spring or summer day, that there are *no* secrets here; unless, of course, you include that age-old secret, *how to catch a trout*. This is a popular spot with stories to tell. And some of those stories *do* include trout to 30 inches.

Grant County is grand country. There are deep valleys between big hills. From the top of one of those hills you will look out on a view that rolls on to forever, or at least as long as vision carries. On blue sky days, there is one landscape; on purple sky, heavy weather days, another. The size of this sky can quickly wash away Montana memories. This is green earth, red barn, black & white cow country. A not-so-still-life with trout.

There are roughly 30 miles of Class II water divided among the three streams. While you are most likely to catch browns—if you catch anything—you could also run into rainbows or occasionally even brookies. Some of the browns are wild, reproducing with success in the clear, cold spring creeks. The Big Green is my favorite, because of the likelihood of catching wild fish, while others rank Castle Rock as tops, because of those behemoths mentioned earlier. The fact is, you could catch a wild brown on Castle Rock or a giant on the Big Green; it's simply a matter of preference. And some folks prefer the Blue, because they think everyone else is on one of its sister streams.

The Approach and the Bait

Since most of your fishing on the Big Green, Castle Rock and the Blue will be without cover of large rocks or substantial vegetation, it is critical to respect the trout's cone of vision, as well as their sensitivity to sound. Approach the stream however you please, but if you do it upright with an anxious gait, you may expect not to catch many fish. The drill is dress the color of the land and the water and the sky, *be quiet!*, stay low. If your neck, back and legs hurt, you are probably low enough. If you are startled by the sound of your own breathing, you are probably being quiet enough.

Now all you have to do is deliver a flawless cast. Unless you are on one of the short, fast-water stretches, a sloppy cast *will* spook the fish. And, yes, it's basic, but don't forget about the shadows cast upon the water by rod and line. There is a great deal to think about. That *is* one of the charms of this kind of fishing, isn't it?

If you must wade, bend over as low as possible and move no faster than the average snail. Do not lift your feet unless absolutely necessary.

The guys who have made a study of these streams will tell you that you can catch fish here on almost anything...as long as it's the right fly, in the right place, at the right time. And you are strongly urged to seek out the advice of anyone who is willing to talk (like there was actually such a thing as a trout fisher who didn't like to talk).

Castle Rock Creek: Narrow, difficult, worth the effort.

A little rain can turn the Blue brown in a matter of minutes.

The flies I've had luck with here make a pretty basic set. First, my favorite, mid-size (8–12) Joe's or Dave's Hoppers. When crickets and hoppers are present and have been dropping onto the water for a day or two, you couldn't make a better choice. My biggest dry-fly fish here came gently (these strikes are seldom gentle) up to a black and brown Dave's Cricket drifted slowly under overhanging grass, sucked it in, then toured the bottom of the river for close to a hundred feet upstream before pivoting and racing straight back at me just to see, I'm convinced of it, if I could strip as fast as she could swim. That was my biggest Big Green trout at the time and the first trout I ever caught that actually was shaped like a football. No, I couldn't fit my hand around her.

Other than hoppers and crickets (do try a black and brown mix), ants can be a good terrestrial choice. Below the surface, size 16 Cress Bugs, with a black flash back, and both size 14 and 16 Fast Sinking Scuds in olive are pretty good bets. Bead-head Pheasant Tails of varying—widely varying—sizes have

We're teaching Wisconsin cows to stay out of the water, but they're exceedingly slow learners.

also worked well. But if I had only one nymph/wet with which to plumb the depths, it would be the Arkansas favorite—a Bead Head Red Ass. On a warm Friday night, fishing a size 16 Red Ass, I took my biggest ever inland Wisconsin trout. The next day, I caught his mom on the same fly.

Up top, small No-hackle BWOs, Sulphurs and PMDs are worth a try, as are size 12 - 16 Deer Hair Caddis. For that matter, any caddis imitation will work sometimes. Just about everyone I've ever talked to about it also recommends Griffith's Gnats for these waters, so you ought to give them a try in spite of my lack of success with them. (Although, I did catch a handsome fish on a red and grizzly Griffith's Gnat-like fly here once. It may have been a fluke, but I had missed several fish on the same fly before finally hooking and landing one.)

Food and Lodging

The bad news is there isn't much to choose from in this area. The good news is that you don't always need a big menu to get a great meal. Fennimore is one of those little Wisconsin towns that looks the same in person as it does on the postcard; neat and tidy, well-scrubbed behind the ears, pleased with itself in a friendly Mayberry sort of way. The folks are decent, and they seem genuinely glad to see you.

I've stayed in a couple of the local motels, and while the Fenmore Hills Motel just west of town on Highway 18 is my usual rest stop, the others were quite acceptable. As for restaurants, well, it's hard to beat The Silent Woman (and the adjoining hotel can make for a great overnight). There is also a fine tavern-cafe-supper-club mix of dining choices, with—to our experience—no clunkers so far.

If you get lucky, you may even hit Fennimore on one of those perfect summer nights when there's music outside downtown and beer and bratwursts and sauerkraut and t housands of silver stars in the black sky. It's always hard to tell on such nights what's best, the music or the food and drink or the fact that you are in a town small enough that you can see the stars from city center.

West Fork Kickapoo River

County: Vernon

Nearest Communities: Avalanche, Westby, Viroqua

Fly/Bait Shop, Guide Service: Avalanche General Store (Avalanche/Viroqua); **Rocking Trout** (Coon Valley); **Spring Creek Angler** (Coon Valley)

Part of the charm of trout streams is that they meander. As we slowly wade upstream and downstream, the wandering side-to-side, back-and-forth, is part of the meditation. If we cannot slow ourselves, the river will slow us. Even where the kayaker or canoeist is sent careening around bends and over rapids, the wading fisher is kept to a cautious pace. It is the nature of trout streams to bob and weave, and the nature of fishers to adjust to the rhythm of the water they're in if they are to stay afoot and catch a fish.

If Wisconsin trout streams are marked by their crookedness, the Kickapoo River is known as the crookedest of them all. I don't know if it's really the crookedest river in Wisconsin or not, but it's pretty crooked. State Highway 131 travels 70 miles from one end of the watershed to the other, crossing the river often. The main stem of the river itself is 120 winding miles from end to end. From the air, it must look like a crazy quilt stitch across the seams of the state's broken fabric.

The Kickapoo has been a river of dreams, a river with and without hope, a river where promises have not always been kept. It is a river that might have been lost to typically poor farming practices, or it might have been lost to yet another dam constructed to protect man from his own ecological misdeeds. There is, to say the least, a sense of mistrust here; a feeling that promises are cheap and easy to break.

Years of overgrazing and farming to the edge in the Coulee Country around the Kickapoo led, as is predictable, to an effect Aldo Leopold compared to "rain on a tin roof." Instead of soaking into the ground as it fell, rain simply ran down the hills, through the valleys and into the river. Flash floods were a common occurrence. To the rescue came the Fed with its standard solution to such problems: a big dam. The idea was pretty much as you'd expect: Build a dam to control flooding, while in the process creating a reservoir that would attract serious tourism dollars to an economically depressed area. For many people living there, the dam and resulting lake were seen as "the answer to our prayers." As a beginning, the government bought and condemned roughly 9,000 acres of land along the river. Then they spent over $18 million getting dam construction started.

But the dam never got built. Environmental concerns won out. Unfortunately, those who saw the dam as their savior felt betrayed. And many who are still in the area remain distrustful of outsiders who come to them with a mouthful of promises. So when Trout Unlimited announced its $370,000 Kickapoo Valley Watershed Conservation Project in late 1998,

it wasn't without a touch of local skepticism. The project was the second of TU's national Home Rivers Initiatives. (New York's Beaverkill-Willowemoc was the first.)

The TU project came to a river, it should be noted, that had already made long strides in coming back thanks to a couple of factors; not the least of which was allowing Mother Nature to do her stuff on these 9,000 "condemned" acres, free of human interference. As much as that part of the waterway has recovered by being left alone, another part of it has been heavily aided in its recovery by caring trout-fishers and other river lovers.

The main stem of the Kickapoo River holds some trout, and as water quality continues to improve, populations are likely to increase. It is the West Fork in Vernon County, however, that receives the most attention from trout-fishers.

Most recent estimates suggest there are close to 1,500 trout per mile on the West Fork. Add in the little tributaries, some with their own healthy populations of big browns and native brookies, and that number could increase substantially.

The character of the West Fork varies somewhat more widely along its roughly 20-mile length than other Coulee Country streams of the southwest corner. To be sure, there are the classic spring creek stretches and short chalk stream runs along limestone walls. There are meadow meanders and wooded bends. There are also freestone riffles and tumbles with too much of their own unique Midwestern charm for the comparisons that are often made to western streams. For the most part wading is easy, though depths can vary dramatically. The latter is most obvious when you think that today is a day hip boots will be sufficient, only to be alerted to the degree of your bad judgment by the thrill of cold spring water caressing your crotch and flowing over the top of the hippers.

What to Fish With

Gear and bait for the West Fork would be as appropriate for other southwest Wisconsin spring creeks. A short rod strung with light-weight, low-visibility line ending in a long, fine leader is usually the best approach. (Although there is one local master who recommends light tackle and tiny flies to others all day then goes out at night with a six-weight outfit coupled to lures big and ugly enough to frighten anything but the largest brown trout. We're talking flies that would give a farm dog a chill. While he doesn't talk much about it, my impression is that the fellow has engineered some remarkable encounters with his dark sorcery.)

The variety of flies I've had success with here is greater

season. My own best fortune has come with a size 16 Elk Hair Caddis and Little Black Caddis in size 18. Light Cahills and Sulphurs from size 14 to 18 have been dependable.

Nothing seems more dependable than the various Blue-Winged Olives. Fished in sizes ranging from 14 to 22 (you have to pay attention to what's in the air, as well as on and in the surface) on gray days, even in light rains, Olives are trout getters. Olives are also one fly where it pays to carry a good variety of sizes *and* styles: Hair wing, hackle tip wing, quill wing, hackle, no hackle, etc.

Hare's Ears, Pheasant Tails and Muskrats from size 10 to 16 make a serviceable basic nymph selection. Scuds and caddis emerger patterns have been known to bring in a fish or two. My own fortune with streamers on the West Fork has not been good, but others recommend black or black and olive Woolly Buggers.

Depending on the weather—sunny, warm and breezy seems best—terrestrials can be great fun. By mid-spring, little black ants are common enough to make occasional trout meals. Cinnamon ants can be good too. As soon as you start seeing crickets, start prospecting with size 12 and 14 Dave's Crickets in a mix of black and brown. By late summer, the

Food and Lodging

The West Fork Sports Club is responsible for (or the center of) much of the good work that has been carried out on the stream. They also manage the West Fork Campground & Cabins in Avalanche at the heart of the West Fork's special regs section. If you're a camper and there's room, you will probably want to look no further.

If you're interested in more amenities, the villages of Westby and Viroqua are both nearby. At Westby, the Old Towne Inn and its adjoining supper club are favorites. Just south of Viroqua, the Hickory Hill Motel has a heated outdoor pool that has often taken the wear out of a long summer day's fishing.

Beside the Old Towne Inn, another fun stop in Westby is the Rod & Gun Club (the only place I know of in dry downtown Westby where you can get a cold beer on a hot summer day. They also operate a nice little campground a ways outside of town on Timber Coulee Creek.) For breakfast, Borgen's Cafe & Bakery is a Westby standard. Viroqua, being a bit larger, offers a larger selection of dining choices, including fast food. Not being particularly fond of fast food, I'd recommend Nate's Supper Club for evening meals.

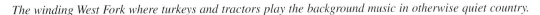

The winding West Fork where turkeys and tractors play the background music in otherwise quiet country.

A perfect dry-fly day, with a 15-inch brown to prove it.
Left: A typical outcome of Wisconsin's wild-trout strategy.

Author at a popular crossing on
the West Fork of the Kickapoo River.

Southwest: West Fork Kickapoo River

Southwest

Coon Creek Watershed

Counties: Vernon, LaCrosse, Monroe
Nearest Communities: Coon Valley, Westby, LaCrosse, Sparta
Fly/Bait Shop, Guide Service: Spring Creek Angler (Coon Valley), Rocking Trout (Coon Valley), Rockin' K Fly Shop (Coon Valley)

Coon Valley is at the heart of Wisconsin's driftless area in the southwest corner. When the last of the glaciers covered Wisconsin 10,000 years ago, this part of the state was, for some reason, left untouched. Opinions as to why this one piece of geography stayed glacier free vary: Some geologists believe the area's mountainous height caused the glacier to go around it. Others have speculated that the area laid below the surface of a great lake and was unglaciated for that reason. More likely the highlands of Upper Michigan and northern Wisconsin slowed the advancing ice of the glacier's Chippewa and Green Bay lobes, and the glacier surrounded the driftless area, but melted before it could be covered.

There is speculation that the melting waters of the last glacier brought the first trout. I believe this because I like the idea, even though there is no overwhelming scientific evidence to support it.

Rolling hills, deep valleys, rock outcrops, miles and miles of clear, cold streams all combine to create some of the most spectacular scenery Wisconsin has to offer. Industry as such is pretty much absent. Farming is the work of choice for many: Dairy and crop farming in particular. Those who don't farm mostly either cater to, or supply, the farmers with a cautious and business-like eye on the tourists who pass through.

Between Coon Valley's self-designation some years back as the *"trout fishing capital of the Midwest"* and, around the same time, Trout Unlimited's naming of Timber Coulee Creek as one of the top 100 trout streams in the country, more than a few of the spring and summer tourists are in Coulee Country to fish.

When I first came to Coon Valley, it was because of stories I had heard from other trout-fishers and because I needed to be in La Crosse (roughly 15 miles away) on business with an associate who fished Coon Creek and the surrounding environs every spring. Essentially, I was anticipating something along the lines of free guide service on a then-foreign piece of water. It seemed like a pretty good deal...at first.

As it turned out, my associate and I were incompatible as fishing partners, so I spent most of my first three days in the area fishing alone. There was a lot of thrashing about, a number of wrong turns and many snags, but those few days ended up being the best fishing trip of any kind I had in years.

On my own, I discovered the simple pleasures of Coon Creek, where it runs through Coon Valley's village park, and north of town in Bohemian Valley. Thanks to a set of good information from the poet, John Judson, who lives in La Crosse, I was introduced to a couple of hiding places for the more difficult-to-catch brown trout of Timber Coulee. Best of all, I was able to put in some true quality time learning to fish with a fly. In the course of that trip, a number of fish were caught, including examples over 12 inches of each trout species present.

It was also on my first trip to Coon Valley that I met Dennis Graupe, the proprietor of the area's first fly shop, Spring Creek Angler. While we've yet to fish together, I've learned a great deal about the Coon Creek watershed and its history from him. Graupe has—with the exception of a year in Alaska—lived no farther away than La Crosse. Most of his years have been spent right there in the valley his family first came to in 1858.

It probably could go without saying that even one good fly shop in an area can make all the difference. On my first visit to Spring Creek Angler, I bought a bunch of the recommended flies, a spool of tippet material, got a free casting lesson on the sidewalk in front of the shop and walked away with an hour's worth of sound advice. On numerous trips back since then, I've always stopped in to pick up a couple "necessary" flies and to check the board to see what and where the action is.

In comparison to some other areas, the Coon Creek watershed doesn't cover a lot of miles by either land or water. If you were to take out your map and draw a box around the most productive part of the watershed—which is *most* of it—that box would be roughly 12 miles top to bottom and a bit over 14 miles across. Even using square miles to make it sound like more, you only come up with between 168 and 172 square miles. If my calculations are correct, there is something over 50 miles of prime water.

(It is only fair to note here that on all four sides of that box we drew above, there are many miles of driftless area trout waters ranging from good to better-than-you-can-imagine. And some of those waters have grown national reputations.)

In addition to Coon Creek itself, some of the other streams that make up the watershed are Bohemian Valley Creek, Timber Coulee Creek, Rullands Coulee Creek and Spring Coulee Creek. You won't have to look or listen too hard before you also take personal note of names such as Poplar, Koll Coulee, Dodson Hollow and Hasley. Even then there are a couple of others locally named or unnamed. You will notice very quickly that creek names roll off the tongues of the locals as though everyone already knew them.

Spring Coulee, where all things are occasionally right with the world.

If you go to Coon Valley and Coon Creek and you haven't been there before, there are things you will notice immediately. Begin with the town of Coon Valley. How many little Midwestern towns, no matter how good the fishing nearby, have a fly shop (and guides) of any kind? And it is also entirely possible that Coon Valley has the best Italian restaurant in the Midwest in Disciascio's. (Any town with a fly shop of Spring Creek Angler's caliber *and* a great Italian restaurant will win me over pretty easily.)

While you're in town, stop at the park. First of all, it's a very pretty park, well groomed and sitting along a beautiful restored stretch of Coon Creek's main branch. It's a great place to picnic and, given the proper permissions, camp. Most notably, the town park offers some of the most attractive, accessible and productive handicap fishing stations I have ever seen.

In the park, you can always find a little stretch of your own to fish, although on the warmest summer days you may need to share the water with kids swimming, tubing and even the occasional canoe. This is one of the places where you are most likely to catch stocked fish. So you are as likely to catch a brook trout here, or a rainbow, as a brown. There are wild fish here, but they share the water with many hatchery fish. Still, the park provides a very pleasant experience, especially when you have children or inexperienced fishers along.

It is even conceivable that you may catch a lunker here. A couple of years ago, I was sitting on the tailgate of the truck, sipping a cold Leinenkugels and deciding where to try next, when a couple of kids—maybe 10 years old—strolled by with a pair of man-size smiles and a trout about as long as their legs. Sure they caught it on corn with an old spin rod, but that didn't diminish the size of the fish one bit.

I particularly like Coon Valley's park at night. A large part of the park along the stream is unlit. Behind you, to the east, the ball park is likely to be lit brightly and noisy from a well-attended game. Across the creek, the opposite bank is lit with hundreds, perhaps thousands, of fireflies. There are more stars in the sky than you can count.

One night, not long ago, as I closed the car door and walked toward the stream, a meteor shower began. Fireflies were everywhere. In the distance to the south, toward Chaseburg, fireworks went off. The glow and the muffled small town roar of America's favorite pastime were at my back. It was a perfect night illuminated by the best light show I've ever seen.

Some nights, fishing Coon Creek in the park or a little ways downstream, large browns can be coaxed out of their lairs to test your skill. The majority may not be lunkers, but you never know.

Much spring-creek fishing is done from a position of prayer.

Spring Coulee Creek (along Spring Coulee Road) is the first long stretch of water running into Coon Creek northeast of town. When you go there, you immediately see some of the other things that set this area apart from many others.

There are pull-offs on both sides of the road. They are there for trout-fishers. There is room for four cars or more here, although given the well-developed sense of courtesy in affect on these streams, you'll seldom see more than two. The stream is well marked with regulation signs on both sides of the road. On both sides of the road there are stiles (ladders) over the fence or split walk-throughs, offering entrance to the private lands where you are welcome to fish. Sometimes, as you cross the fence onto his or her land, the landowner will see you and smile and wave. In few places is the level of respect and acceptance so high. This is true of more water than not in the Coon Creek watershed.

Spring Coulee offers a variety of experiences. The landscape varies from wide meadow and pasture stream to narrow stretches, thick with brush. All of it is good wild brown trout water. There is also rainbow and brook trout too, though only in small numbers these days. There is a classic mix of bends and switchbacks, straight runs, fast and slow water, deep and shallow water.

A few miles north of Spring Coulee Creek, Coon Creek flows out of a stretch also known as Bohemian Valley Creek. Here, at the intersection of County Highways P and G, Timber Coulee Creek enters from the east. This is fine and very interesting water.

Heading up into Bohemian Valley, along County G, tall vegetation, along with the stream's shape and size can make casting a challenge for some of us. The fish are spooky too. Even the occasional rainbow will extend his hook-free life by seeing you well before you see him. You need to sneak. You need to be quiet. You need to stay low. The streams of the Coon Creek watershed are geared more to quiet stalkers than those who announce their presence with their every move and gesture. Even the dumb fish are only *so* dumb.

If you follow CTH P along Timber Coulee Creek rather than turning up toward Bohemian Valley, you will come upon a variety of accessible stretches of the area's best known water. This is also where you will find the single artificials-only section in the Coon Creek watershed.

A lot of restoration work has been done on Timber Coulee, above and extending down into the artificals-only section. That work has, in some places, changed the nature of the stream. As you might guess, these changes are controversial. Old-timers say it was perfect as it was. All that was needed was more control over wading cattle. Others say "improvements," including longer stretches of faster water, create an overall more productive environment. High hopes and great expectations are held out in particular for the "Bob Jackson" area, so named for a local trout and stream champion.

More History

It is so easy to be a critic of change. Especially when something is already good. It was change, however, monumental change, that turned the Cook Creek Watershed into what we have today.

Two events stand out from all others in creating this place as we know it. The first was in the fall of 1933 when the US Department of Interior Soil Erosion Service established Project #1 at Coon Valley. The second occurred when Irvin Larson, Harold Tune and Kenneth Graupe (Dennis Graupe's father) brought their tractors and other implements of construction to Timber Coulee Creek at the Snowflake Ski area, at the behest of the Westby Rod & Gun Club, to begin trout habitat improvement work in May of 1962.

With the Soil Erosion Service establishment of Project #1 in 1933, Civilian Conservation Corps workers moved in, and work began in May of 1934. As one local history describes the project, "Cooperative agreements were signed with farmers living within the boundaries of the Coon Creek Watershed to remember this well, because my father had his own tractor, chain saw, log chain and so on from home to help put structures in the streams. They put in 90 log wing deflectors—which had lots of overhead cover for big trout—from the ski hill down to the Olstad bridge. The hatchery trucks rolled in and thousands of brown trout were stocked.

"Because of all the chubs and minnows still in the creeks, the trout grew to spectacular weights and lengths, and numbers. It was during the early '60s things began coming together for Timber Coulee Creek."

The road into the Westby Rod & Gun Club campground.

above the park in Coon Valley since 1989. "They were last stocked in Timber Coulee Creek in 1986." Rainbows are stocked in Coon Creek at Coon Valley and in Bohemian Valley (some of these latter have grown to the 15 to16 inch range).

When the subject of brook trout comes up, Vetrano is enthusiastic. He would clearly like to see more done with brook trout in the area. This includes stocking as well as the possibility of restrictive regulations to bring them back in streams and tributaries that are now clear and clean enough to support them.

The emphasis in what Vetrano is saying is on wild brook trout. He talks about the success of wild brown trout transfers and discusses his hopes for similar transfers with wild brookies. As this book was written, experimental stockings of wild brook trout in some driftless area streams had begun. So far, brook trout reintroductions appear to be successful.

Today there are few pieces of water that provide better fishing than the streams of the driftless area. The Coon Creek Watershed is a gem among gems. Responsible use can keep it that way; clear thinking with an eye to the future can make it even better. When you go, be gentle. Tread lightly. Respect what you find and the good works that have been done up to this point.

Current Management

In the years since that monumental stream work, a lot has happened. Some of it good, some bad. Floods in 1978 and 1983 were disastrous. Lunker structures, sometimes criticized as "small trout structures," replaced washed-out wing deflectors.

Largely as a result of everything that has happened, the Coon Creek Watershed, notably Timber Coulee Creek, has remained healthy and productive. Enough so to be considered a trout nursery by the Wisconsin DNR, capable of yielding enough small trout to be removed for planting elsewhere. But this begs the question, "Why stock hatchery fish into a

Finding Your Way

The Coon Creek Watershed lies mainly in Vernon County, but extends into LaCrosse and Monroe counties to the north and northeast. The main highways of the immediate area are 14 and 61 traveling east-west, 162 coming into Coon Valley from the north and south, and 27 coming into Westby from the north and south. There are many other roads with excellent stream access that you will discover as you explore.

Kinnickinnic River

Counties: **St. Croix, Pierce**
Nearest Communities: **River Falls, Hudson, St. Paul, Minneapolis, Stillwater**
Fly/Bait Shop, Guide Service: **Lund's Hardware** (River Falls); **Bob Mitchell's Fly Shop** (Lake Elmo, MN)

There are trout-fishers who wax nostalgic or drift off uncontrollably at first mention of the "Kinni." Maybe it's because it's two of the finest trout streams in the United States—to say nothing of where it ranks among Wisconsin trout waters. Or maybe it's because even after the devastating effects of drought, heavy pressure from catch-and-keep fishers, careless land management practices and, some would say, criminal discharge of pollutants and poisons, it still supports a naturally reproducing brown and brook trout population of several thousand fish per mile. Maybe it's simply because there is nothing *not* to like about fishing through or just outside of such a pleasant, little, farm country, university town as River Falls. (More on the latter later.) Whatever the reason, the Kinni is a favorite among all of those who have fished it; and being less than an hour's drive east of the twin cities of Minneapolis-St. Paul, it *has* been fished by many.

All of this is not to say that the river is easy to fish. I probably ought to be embarrassed to admit that I fished the Kinni several times over two summers before I caught even one fish there. I had read stories about it being the most heavily populated (with fish) trout streams in Wisconsin, but my first experiences indicated that the trout had packed their little fish bags and moved on to parts unknown. By contrast, more recent seasons on the Kinni produced both the most and the biggest fish I've ever caught there. It is a river well worth learning.

A River to Defend

The Kinnickinnic River wanders for some 22 miles of Class I water down and across St. Croix and Pierce counties to the state line, where it flows into the St. Croix River. It has been a long time since the Kinni could have been considered a secret, but it is more recently that the valleys of the St. Croix and Kinnickinnic became the rustic bedroom of Minneapolis-St. Paul. This is still beautiful country, and the little communities of River Falls and Hudson have not lost their charm, but things *are* becoming crowded. Overdevelopment *is* a concern.

Enter the Kinnickinnic River Land Trust, a member-supported conservation organization that works in partnership with landowners, farmers, other organizations and businesses to permanently protect the watershed from the dangers of uncontrolled residential growth. The Trust works to gain conservation easements that will prevent sprawl now and in the future. The Trust doesn't own the protected lands, but rather assumes a responsibility to ensure that restrictions to damaging growth are observed by all future land owners.

Doug Swisher, in encouraging support for the Trust, says: "The Kinnickinnic is one of my favorite spring creeks. It has everything you could ask for. It is challenging, scenic, productive and easily accessible. It was the home of my early fly fishing schools...It is frightening to think how dramatically it will change if development continues unchecked."

The Two Rivers

Above River Falls, in St. Croix County, the Kinni is a cold, meandering ribbon, maybe 25 feet across at its widest. Wading is easy through this stretch, though one needs to be

Late-afternoon nymphing along a deep bend in the Kinni.

aware that careless short people may find themselves in over their waders in a hurry. Much of the bank is brush or tree lined. The bottom is largely sand. (And, yes, there is some muck.) Casting, for the most part, is relatively easy. There are spots, however, where fly fishing is difficult at best. I have found the fish spooky here, although others have told me how easy they are to catch. Since experience is as good a guide as any, I'd suggest fishing with a short, light rod, long leaders and flies ranging from small to microscopic. The upper Kinni is one of those places where I've often thrown cast after cast to the fishiest-looking spots, become convinced no fish were present, then plodded into a pod of big browns, spooking them madly upstream and guaranteeing failure for much of the rest of a day or evening. Estimates of fish numbers in the upper river range from 8,000 to as high 10,000 fish per mile.

Below River Falls, through the canyon in Pierce County, the Kinni is a freestoner with cobble and boulders, deep bends, shallow riffles, strong currents and bigger—if fewer—fish (maybe 4,000 per mile). Thanks (unfortunately) to runoff and dams, water temperatures are a bit higher than upstream, and trout may dine on minnows and other meat not as available up where the water runs cold. Many of the fishers I've met prefer the upper Kinni, but this, the lower end, is my favorite. I like the way it looks, the way it feels. I like the fish I catch here now that I have finally learned how to catch them. This is the way a trout stream should be: The canyon walls are a bonus.

Of all the places I have fished alone, the lower Kinni is my favorite lonely place. Considering the proximity of a couple million city-dwellers and another hundred thousand of their bedroom cousins, one can be amazingly by one's self down here. It probably has something to do with those canyon walls. Come sometime between Tuesday morning and Thursday afternoon, and you are likely to find the Kinnickinnic State Park parking lot just north of the intersection of County Trunks F and FF completely empty. However one measures the quality of alone-ness, this place can be off the scales on a perfect day.

What To Fish With

Begin with the basics. Adams (16–18), Elk Hair Caddis (14–18), Little Black Caddis (18–20), Blue-Winged Olives (16–22), Griffith's Gnats (22) in traditional form, as well as red and grizzly, Pheasant Tails (14–16), Muskrats (14–16) and Prince Nymphs (12–18). No-hackle flies are most dependable in all but the fastest water. My own success with streamers here is limited, but Little Brook Trout, Little Brown Trout, Black Nose Dace and Sculpins all stand some chance of producing fish.

Food, Lodging, Entertainment

This area is a treat. If you want to fish then move to the full-blown city experience, swing over to the Twin Cities for hotels, music, theater, fine restaurants, trendy bars and maybe even a St. Paul Saints baseball game. (The latter being a five-star experience, highly recommended to everyone.)

Sometimes mid-stream fly redesign is a necessity.
Left: The Kinnickinnic proves that fast-water canyon
fishing is readily available in Wisconsin.

On the other hand, if you would like to enjoy your non-fishing hours with a few less lights and a little less noise, stay close to the river. For lodging, both River Falls and Hudson offer as much variety as anyone could wish for, from camping to bed & breakfasts to well-scrubbed chain motels. Personal favorite: The Hudson House (Best Western) in Hudson.

Your food choices are equally diverse. One of the advantages to being the bedroom of a major metropolitan area is that you often won't need to go into the city to get a good meal. For burgers and beers, I like Bo's & Mine in downtown River Falls. Or you can get a terrific pizza at Luigi's, just a couple of blocks down the street.

If shopping during your non-fishing hours is of interest, River Falls, Hudson and Stillwater, Minnesota, just to the north, offer a variety of shops. Antique hunters will find themselves particularly at home here. Non-traditional sidetrips might include a Kansas City Chiefs' practice session in River Falls during training camp (between late July and mid-August), an excursion boat trip up and down the St. Croix or a hot air balloon flight over the Kinnickinnic and St. Croix River valleys.

Finding Your Way

To get to the Kinni, simply take a left (head south) off of Interstate 94 at Highway 65. From 94 to River Falls, 65 parallels the river, and other roads offering access along the way are obvious. Below River Falls, access is not so readily found. Best bet is to take County FF west to County F, head north across the river and park in the State Park lot (you will need a State Park decal or sticker to show you have paid your dues for leaving your vehicle here). From this point, you may wade as far up and down stream as you please.

West Central

Willow River

Counties: **St. Croix, Pierce**
Nearest Communities: **River Falls, Hudson, St. Paul, Minneapolis, Stillwater**
Fly/Bait Shop, Guide Service: **Lund's Hardware** (River Falls); **Bob Mitchell's Fly Shop** (Lake Elmo, MN)

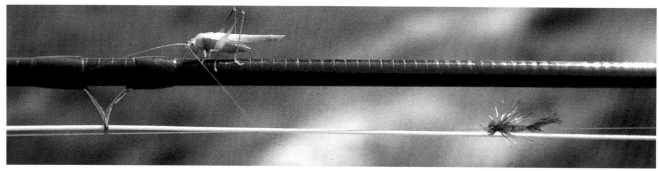

Above: Time to change flies?
Right: Floyd Halla demonstrates that short-line nymphing can be a winning tactic on the Willow.

On a perfect late-summer day, my brother and I walked along a riverside trail in Willow River State Park looking for a piece of water with *TROUT* written all over it. Our conversation, or perhaps merely our presence, startled two squawking great blue herons into the air. When we looked up, in the same small patch of blue sky, we also saw two soaring bald eagles. I've often seen eagles and herons along the same stretch of river, but never such a congregation in such a small area. It wasn't hard to figure out what all the big birds were doing there, being as close to breakfast time as it was, so we slipped as quietly as possible into the water. (The trail we had been walking is designated the Trout Brook Trail. How could you not fish in such a place?)

A River in Flux

There are between 25 and 30 miles of Class I, II and III trout water in the Willow. Both browns and rainbows, mostly put here by the DNR, sometimes grow to substantial size over a couple of years. There was a time, not all that long ago, when this was one of our most heavily fished streams. Fish grew large. Creels were easy to fill. Perhaps the latter is one of the reasons why fishers have been complaining for the past few years that "the fishin' ain't what it used to be."

I'm reminded of a chance meeting with a fellow who complained that the fishing wasn't that good anymore. He reminisced how he had come down to his favorite hole for years taking two or three fish a day for breakfast or for dinner, or for the freezer. And how it seemed like every year there were fewer and smaller fish. He wondered out loud, "Where the hell did they go?!?"

There is ongoing debate as to how much Willow River fishing has deteriorated. General agreement is that things have

gone downhill over the last three decades, but many believe that lately fishing has gotten better, and that recent dam removals can only make things better yet. My own recommendation would be to take a couple of days, and try it for yourself. The Willow is in a state of flux, but it may also be in a state of flex. Given time, there is no reason for hopes not to be high.

Fishers used to think of the Willow as dry-fly water, and certainly it still has its days. Come with a good selection of crayfish, sculpin and Muddler patterns, however, as well as the usual dries and nymphs, and you will be much better prepared for the unexpected.

Apres fish

The nearest communities to the Willow River are Hudson, Wisconson and Stillwater, Minnesota, both mentioned earlier under the Kinnickinnic River. Both offer excellent lodging, especially if you're looking for a B&B. Both offer a fine range of dining choices. Both offer plenty of small town, downtown charm. For beginners, consider cocktails at Riverside (in Hudson), overlooking the St. Croix River, at sunset. (You'll find they also serve up terrific lunches and dinners). If you like Italian, give Mama Maria's a try.

You won't have a problem finding a place to eat in Stillwater either, but if you would like a great view to go with your meal, try The Dock overlooking the river. Instead of having dessert there, wander downtown to Tremblay's Homemade Fudge & Chocolates for a piece of fudge (and a bag of hard candy for the ride home).

Rush River

County: **Pierce**
Nearest Communities: **El Paso, River Falls, Menomonie, Eau Claire**
Fly/Bait Shop, Guide Service: **Lund's Hardware** (River Falls)**; Scheel's All Sports** (Eau Claire)

I had just returned home from a few days of wandering back and forth between the Kinnickinnic and Rush rivers, having particularly good fortune on both. I hadn't caught as many fish on the Rush, but they were bigger, both in length and in girth. There was no reason not to be happy with myself. Until, that is, about half way through a conversation with an acquaintance from Minnesota who spends a lot of time fishing western Wisconsin. He's a pleasant enough fellow, but when he referred to fishing the Rush as "fishing in an aquarium," I took umbrage. The Rush is a river that clearly illustrates how much opinions can vary.

Some fishers love the Rush for its perfect setting and large—sometimes very large—trout. Others stay away, because most of those big fish have grown from planted stocks, or because of the crowds they have sometimes encountered on the river. It seems no two people can agree on the best fishing spot either. And one person's favorite will almost certainly be cause for disdain by someone else. True, the vast majority of those really big fish started out as stockers, but it took some stream time to grow that big. And, yes, there are a couple of bridge crossings and parking areas on the Rush that are always crowded; and we *do* mean crowded, but, with the exception of opening weekend, you can almost always find a place to be by yourself.

What To Fish With

You can come to the Rush with a standard selection of flies that work all over Wisconsin, or you can add a few twists and maybe catch more and/or bigger fish. Certainly Blue-Winged Olives, from size 16 to 20, to cover both varieties, are always a good bet. Caddis Emergers, Pheasant Tails and Hare's Ears from size 10 to 16 will also provide consistent results. Deer Hair and other caddis patterns in a wide range of sizes are a staple all season. Mid-summer can deliver some exciting Trico hatches, if you're ready for them. Very small (size 20-22) Cream Midges are good mid-to-late summer.

On the other hand, you could veer from the norm and try something like a size 12 Bitch Creek. Bitch Creeks don't get fished much in Wisconsin, but there are streams where they do work...and this is one of them. It may be appropriate, given the time Doug Swisher spent in this part of Wisconsin, but his Madame X has also turned out to be a strong performer on the Rush. Both of these flies are worth a few casts if you're looking for the biggest Rush River trout, say, those between 20 and 30 inches. Or you could confine your angling to early morning and late evening and do it all with your favorite Deer Hair Mouse.

Food, Lodging and Entertainment

River Falls (mentioned earlier) is nearby, and staying there does put you in closer proximity to the Kinnickinnic and Willow, should you choose to fish those rivers as well as the Rush during your stay. For something a little different, however, you might want to consider staying in Menomonie.

Menomonie has several motels and B&Bs. My favorite place to stay there is a unique combination of the two, the Bolo Country Inn. The Bolo was once a motel, but the people who run it treat each room more like it was a bed and breakfast, complete with wine upon arrival and a breakfast basket delivered to your door in the morning.

On Menomonie's Main Street, you'll find the Mabel Tainter Memorial Building. Built in 1889, the building houses the public library, a theater arts museum and, of greatest note, a theater where local productions are staged. If at all possible, put an evening at the Mabel Tainter Theater on your after-fishing schedule.

As for food, well, there are several very good places to eat in or near Menomonie, but my favorite restaurant in all of Wisconsin is only a few miles south in Downsville. The Creamery is housed in, yes, an old creamery building. In spite of its rural setting and casual atmosphere, the Creamery can compete with some of the finest restaurants in the country. It is a local favorite that also draws from Minneapolis-St. Paul. The setting is perfect, the gardens a delight and the food good enough to make you forget all of the Creamery's other charms. The experience can be almost magical. (As a bonus, Dunn County Pottery is housed in the same building.)

Where the River Lies

The Rush River bubbles up out of the ground somewhere in the vicinity of Interstate 94 and runs all the way south to the Mississippi River, crossing Highways 29, 63, 72, 10 and 35 in the process. There are well-known hot spots at Martell and El Paso.

The Rush offers good fishing throughout the season.
Inset: If you're ever in El Paso, check this place out.

Bois Brule River

Northwest

County: Douglas
Nearest Communities: Brule, Superior, Hayward
Fly/Bait Shop, Guide Service: Angler's All (Ashland);
    Brule River Classics (Brule); Superior Fly
    Anglers (Superior)

There is strong argument for calling the Bois Brule the most famous river in Wisconsin. Having been fished by Grant, Cleveland, Hoover, Coolidge and Eisenhower (as well as a spy or two, and a handful of other famous and infamous types), it is rightly called "the river of presidents." Undammed, it is a free-flowing, wild river. Holding a population of brookies, browns, rainbows, steelhead and salmon, it could be considered nothing short of trout rich.

Yet there are the detractors. There are those who say, "It ain't what it used to be." So what is? Then there are those who say the salmon (wanderers from Canadian introductions) have ruined the steelhead runs of old (the jury's still out, though something appears to be awry). Those who bemoan the loss of the "coasters" (the big, lake-run brook trout were long gone before most of us were born, thanks to market fishermen and a handful of greedy bastards who thought the resource was their own private stock). And those, like one popular fishing show host, who have dubbed the river "Cruel Brule" in memory of their own lack of success. (Cruel Brule, Bitter Brule: If these characters were a little less full of themselves and could simply observe and digest simple instruction, they would catch fish.)

The Bois Brule may not be what it was once upon a time,

but it is still a great river. Try to tell a kid who has just caught an eight-inch brook trout or a codger with a hefty steelhead at the end of a taut, throbbing line that it isn't, and they will share with you their personal truths.

Which Brule?

A standard point of confusion necessary to point out here is that Wisconsin is the home to *two* Brules. They are both at the northern end of the state, the border Brule on the east, the Bois Brule on the west. They are rivers of completely disparate characters. Even their names come from distinct sources. As if to feed the fire of confusion, those who adore the Bois Brule insist upon calling it simply "the Brule." Tip: When you get where you're going, know where you are. There have been more than a few anglers who fished the one thinking it was the other.

Points of Fact, Historical and Otherwise

Before the arrival of European explorers, the Bois Brule served as a link between the Mississippi and Lake Superior. Other whites may have come earlier, but Daniel Greysolon, Sieur du Lhut (for whom Duluth, Minnesota was named) was the first to record his journey for the edification of others. It is

A fall-run male steelhead.

MATT & LAURIE SUPINSKI

93

MATT & LAURIE SUPINSKI

A fat silver Bois Brule coho.

also possible that Etienne Brule may have paddled the river, but he is *not* the source of the river's name. (Bois brule is French for "burned wood," an indicator that forest fires preceded those who named the river.) The standard cadre of fur traders and missionaries weren't far behind.

A steelhead paradise for those who make the long climb down.

From its headwaters in the pine barrens of Douglas County to its mouth at Lake Superior, there are almost 50 miles of Class I trout water to the Brule. This is a river that may once, a long time ago, have flowed both north *and* south. Yes, it sounds absurd, but how could you not enjoy the image of a river flowing two directions at once? And besides, it may be true. Such a phenomena could help explain why, even without being cursed by a dam, the Brule is still very much a river of two quite unique personalities. The upper river ambles slowly (for the most part) down to US Highway 2 at Brule, then not far north, begins rumbling, tumbling its rocky coarse to the skull-numbing cold of Superior.

The upper river is fed by numerous springs which provide a constant source of clear, cold water to the Brule. This part of the river falls at a rate of three feet per mile for its first 30 miles. Then, when it crosses the "Copper Range," it begins a fall of 328 feet in the remaining 19 miles.

The fish here are native brookies, wild browns and rainbows, naturally reproducing steelhead and coho salmon. The numbers of each are open to debate (and all of the rainbows *may* be anadromous), but they are sufficient.

Resident brookies will usually be found upstream of Highway 2. You are also very likely to find quite a few browns and some rainbows in the upper river. Lake-run browns begin to enter the river as early as late July and will continue through September (and beyond, depending on the weather). Steelhead come up the river beginning in September and over-winter, spawning in spring. A second steelhead run starts in March.

At the upper end of the river, you may paddle and wade your way to your stopping point, with most of the paddling relatively easy. At the lower end, you pick an access point, say a prayer and wade with extreme care into "the other river."

How and What To Fish

If you expect to do the most thorough possible job of fishing the Brule, your basic equipment will need to include a couple of rods between four- and eight-weight, a good selection of dries, nymphs and streamers, as well as some lowly egg patterns, a belt cinched tight, a wading staff, a flashlight, patience, a sense of humor *and* a canoe. You will also want to talk to everyone you can find who has fished the river about what worked when and where and what didn't. You don't just come up here and start flailing around expecting to catch a trout. This is *not* easy water. This is special water...to some, even sacred.

The Brule hosts excellent hatches. Beginning in late April or early May, Hendricksons (size 12–14) will come off and continue to emerge through Memorial Day. Sulphurs (size 14–18) will make their late afternoon appearance through June. The brown drakes (size 8–10) arrive from sunset to dark through June. March browns can be expected to appear from late May into July. Later in June, come prepared for what can be a very good Hex hatch—and, according to Brule guide, Ron Manz, "the Brule has some super daytime Hex hatches," for which "very realistic dun patterns" are just the thing. Through August and September, Tricos (size 20–22) are a good morning bet. Blue-winged olives (size 16–24) will appear sometime in summer and last until sometime in fall. It's tempting to call BWOs the "forever" fly, because, given gray weather, they seem always to be present from mid-to-late

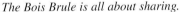

The Bois Brule is all about sharing.

The Bois Brule requires cautious wading...preceded by prayer.

afternoon all season and beyond. Caddis in various patterns, sizes and colors appear throughout the season.

Ants, beetles and spiders (try a size 16 Brown or Black Bivisible, and see what happens) are always good bets on the upper river once summer kicks in. On the lower river, all of the above may work, but also consider throwing Mickey Finns, Black Nose Dace, Little Rainbows, Little Brookies, Woolly Buggers, Black Stoneflies and the Manz Ostrich Herl Leech. If egg patterns don't offend your sensibilities, you could find those quite successful too.

Finding Your Way

The Bois Brule lies east of Highway 53 and is more or less paralleled by 27 up to 2 at Brule. From 2 north, the river runs between H and 13 on the east and Clevedon Road on the west. Pull-offs and criss-crossing trails between the two make easy access all the way to Lake Superior.

The Brule River Sportsmen's Club (Box 48, Brule, WI 54820) publishes an excellent map of the lower Bois Brule. Steelheaders should not take to the stream without it.

When You Aren't Fishing

In the tiny community of Brule, you will find all the basics in what the travel books call "gas, food, lodging." If you're looking for a bed, try to book one of the cabins at Brule River Classics (they also have an excellent fly shop and can hook you up with a guide). You can get fed at both the local cafe and the local tavern (depending on time of day). And, if you don't have a canoe of your own, you can rent one in Brule. As long as you can live simply, you will do fine right here.

Should your needs require more options, consider overnighting in Hayward. Hayward's a fine, fun little northwoods city with just enough of everything: restaurants, taverns, motels, shops, even a casino. And while in Hayward, don't miss a visit to the Freshwater Fishing Hall of Fame where you can view record fish, fishing memorabilia and antique outboard motors, *and* stand in the jaws of a four-story high muskie. There are certain things it's very difficult to pass up.

Namekagon River

Counties: **Bayfield, Sawyer**
Nearest Communities: **Hayward, Cable**
Fly/Bait Shop, Guide Service: **Anglers All** (Ashland);
    Brule River Classics (Brule); **Pastika's** (Hayward)

I don't know this river as well as I would like. I've fished it only a few times. But it is a river I often see in dreams. You know the kind of dreams I mean; the kind where you dream of a trout stream you don't know, but it looks perfect, and you catch a lot of big fish. Or you catch a lot of fish. Or you catch a big fish. And your company is the one person you want to be with, or no one. This is the Namekagon. The look alone sucks you in. It could be fish free, and you would slam on your brakes to fish for trout here. There are not as many trout—especially naturally reproducing trout—as we would wish, but there are trout, and some of them are remarkably large...or so I'm told. (Yes, I have seen pictures to back up the big-fish stories.)

There are a little over 20 miles of Class I and II trout water here. The trout waters officially begin at Hayward, but trout (stocked and not) do occur below that favorite Wisconsin tourist town. Natural reproduction takes place, but it is limited. Brook trout appear more in and near tributary streams. Rainbows are peppered throughout the stream. Browns, wary and growing to substantial size, are often the target of choice. The size of the largest of them helps to make up for the low populations.

Nothing comes easy on the Namekagon. You'll need to work for whatever you get. This is not the wild, cold, relatively free-running stream it could and should be. Thanks to the National Wild and Scenic Rivers Act, an act designed to protect and preserve, the Namekagon is protected and preserved in the same degraded state it was in when the Act was passed in 1968: That is, a river beaten, battered and dammed by logging interests and beavers. Our hope is that eventually reason will prevail and true restoration and preservation work will be done here. In the meantime, the Namekagon has remained a big, classically beautiful river that hosts a respectable number of trout, including what may be a unique strain of browns able to withstand even warmer temperatures than browns normally can.

How and What To Fish With

The Namekagon is a wide river—over a hundred feet across at its widest—where casting and wading is a breeze. It's best fished at the beginning or end of the season, although a few dedicated summer anglers who hit the water during the earliest morning and latest evening hours, and have practiced their craft here often, do report finding the big browns agreeable targets.

Thanks to all that room, casting up-and-across or down-and-across is much easier here than on many Wisconsin trout streams. If you fish early morning, late evening or the deepest

Where the Namekagon begins.

Morning on the Namekagon.

holes any time of day, throwing streamers across-and-down can be effective. Sculpin, Maribou Leech and Little Brook, Brown or Rainbow Trout patterns all have possibilities, as do some of the larger Black or Brown Stoneflies. Your best bet is to try a variety of sizes, but you may as well go in with high hopes, using the biggest streamers in your box first.

Prince Nymphs, Pheasant Tails, Copper Bobs, March Browns, Hare's Ears and Muskrats from size 12 down to size 16 can all be the right fly at the right time. For dries, stick with the standards to begin with. Blue-Winged Olives from size 14 to 20 are a necessity, as well as a full cadre of Adams variations. In particular, you may want to try a Female Adams with a nice fluffy yellow ass. I've also had some action here with Rich Osthoff's Duck Shoulder Duns in sizes 14 and 16. If you are on the water from late spring to mid summer, you might also encounter one of several healthy Sulphur hatches. Tricos can be expected in the air for late-season early risers.

Eat, Sleep, Amuse Yourself

Hayward, mentioned earlier, makes an excellent base of operations for Namekagon fishers. So does Cable toward the northern end of the river. There are motels and campgrounds aplenty. My suggestion, unless you arrive at the high point of the tourist season, is to take a drive along the river, see what appeals to you, and experiment with the charm and hospitality of northern Wisconsin.

The River and the Road

Highway 63 tracks the Namekagon north to just short of Cable. At Cable, you can poke at the river here and there by turning east on County M, pulling off at the obvious pull-offs and experimenting with the side roads.

Very large dragonfly in Cable.

Fly Patterns, Hatches and Flies

Many, if not most, of the flies mentioned herein and shown in the photographs are common to the entire United States and are tied pretty much the same way everywhere. A few of the best-known flies were developed by Wisconsin tiers. Others are less well-known or are tied differently in other states or regions. And then there are those that are truly unique to Wisconsin.

(Although most of the latter do seem to work just about any place you go.)

The recipes that follow are for those flies that are tied with a unique twist in Wisconsin and those that were either developed or are fished almost exclusively in the Badger State. The common flies are found in many books and videos, and are readily available commercially.

Henryville Special
Hook: Standard dry fly, sizes 14–18
Thread: Dark tan
Rib: Grizzly hackle
Body: Olive dubbing
Underwing: Barred wood duck
Overwing: Mallard quill sections
Hackle: Ginger

Cap's Hairwing/Hairwing Adams (Cap Buettner and Ed Haaga)
Hook: Standard dry fly, sizes 12–18
Thread: Black
Tail: Deer hair
Rib: Black thread
Body: Deer hair
Wing: Deer hair
Hackle: Brown and grizzly

DSD Blue-Winged Olive (Rich Osthoff)
Hook: Standard dry fly, sizes 14–20
Thread: Light olive
Tail: Olive or gray hackle fibers
Body: Olive-gray dubbing
Wings: Dun duck shoulder feathers

DSD Sulphur (Rich Osthoff)
Hook: Standard dry fly, sizes 18–22
Thread: Light gray
Tail: Sulphur hackle fibers
Body: Sulphur dubbing
Wings: Light dun duck shoulder feathers

DSD March Brown (Rich Osthoff)
Hook: Standard dry fly, sizes 12–16
Thread: Tan
Tail: Tan hackle fibers
Body: Tan dubbing
Wings: Dun duck shoulder feathers

Upland Caddis (Rich Osthoff)
Hook: Standard dry fly, sizes 12–16
Thread: Dark tan
Body: Dark brown dubbing
Hackle: Brown
Wings: Ruffed grouse back
Antennae: Green feather stem butts

Pass Lake
Hook: Standard dry fly, sizes 14–18
Thread: Black
Tail: Mallard flank fibers
Body: Peacock herl
Wing: White calf hair
Hackle: Brown

White Wolf/Wulff
Hook: Standard dry fly, sizes 10–14
Thread: Gray
Tail: White bucktail
Body: Cream dubbing
Wing: White calf hair
Hackle: White or light badger

Hornberg (Frank Hornberg)
Hook: Standard dry fly, sizes 10–14
Thread: Black
Body: Silver tinsel
Underwing: Deer hair
Overwing: Mallard flank feathers
Cheek: Jungle cock
Hackle: Grizzly

Renegade
Hook: Standard dry fly, sizes 12–18
Tag: Gold tinsel
Thread: Black
Hackle: Brown
Body: Peacock herl
Hackle: White

Prince Nymph
Hook: Standard nymph, sizes 10–14
Thread: Black
Tail: Pheasant tail fibers
Body: Peacock herl (over weighted wire)
Wings: White goose biots
Hackle: Soft brown hackle

Copper Bob (Robert White)
Hook: Standard or 2X nymph, sizes 12–18
Thread: Black or brown
Tail: Pheasant tail fibers
Body: Copper wire
Thorax: Peacock or dubbing to match wire
Wing case: Pheasant or turkey

Soft Hackle Wooly (Rich Osthoff)
Hook: Standard or 2X nymph, sizes 12–16
Thread: Black
Tail: Black rabbit fur
Body: Black rabbit dubbed (over weighted wire)
Hackle: Grizzly hen neck

Fast-Sinking Scud (Rich Osthoff)
Hook: Standard nymph, sizes 10–18
Thread: Olive
Tail: Quail or woodcock feather fibers
Shell: Clear elastic or "Scudback"

Rib: 4X or 5X tippet material
Underbody: Punch embroidery yarn (over weighted wire)
Body: Olive-gray rabbit and antron dubbing
Legs: Teased out dubbing

Bi-Bugger (Rich Osthoff)
Hook: 2X nymph, sizes 4–12
Thread: Black

Tail: Black rabbit fur with flash
Underbody: Black punch embroidery yarn (over weighted wire)
Body: Black rabbit and Antron Dubbing
Hackle: Grizzly hen hackle

Little Brown Trout
Hook: Standard streamer, sizes 4–14

Thread: Brown
Tail: Bucktail
Body: White fur dubbing
Rib: Gold tinsel
Wing: Yellow bucktail, orange bucktail, gray squirrel tail, red squirrel tail, barred badger

Wisconsin Hatch Chart

	Jan	Feb	Mar	Apr	May	Jun	Jul	Aug	Sep	Oct	Nov	Dec
Caddisflies												
Grannom				▓	▓	▓						
Little Black				▓	▓	▓						
Green						▓	▓	▓				
Mayflies												
Blue-Winged Olive			▓	▓	▓	▓	▓	▓	▓	▓		
Hendrickson				▓	▓							
Sulphur					▓	▓	▓					
Light Cahill						▓	▓	▓				
Gray Drake					▓	▓						
Brown Drake						▓						
Hexagenia						▓	▓					
Tiny Blue-Winged Olive						▓	▓	▓	▓			
Trico							▓	▓	▓			
White Mayfly								▓				
Midges												
		▓	▓	▓	▓	▓	▓	▓	▓	▓	▓	
Stoneflies												
Yellow Sally					▓	▓						
Black			▓									
Brown							▓					
Golden						▓						
Terrestrials												
Ants					▓	▓	▓	▓	▓	▓		
Crickets					▓	▓	▓	▓	▓	▓		
Grasshoppers							▓	▓	▓	▓		
Spiders						▓	▓	▓	▓	▓		
Beetles					▓	▓	▓	▓	▓	▓		

Drys

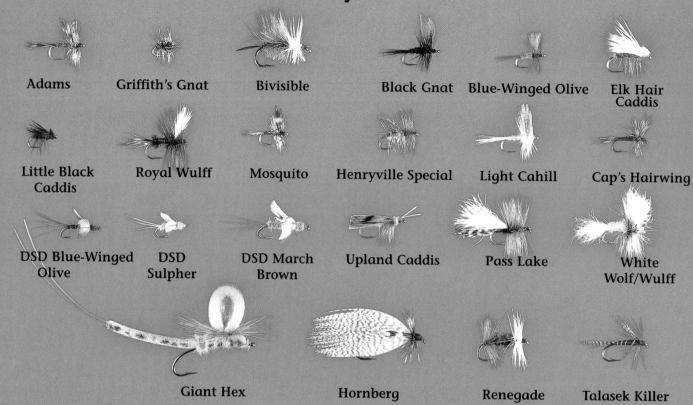

Adams	Griffith's Gnat	Bivisible	Black Gnat	Blue-Winged Olive	Elk Hair Caddis
Little Black Caddis	Royal Wulff	Mosquito	Henryville Special	Light Cahill	Cap's Hairwing
DSD Blue-Winged Olive	DSD Sulpher	DSD March Brown	Upland Caddis	Pass Lake	White Wolf/Wulff

Giant Hex   Hornberg   Renegade   Talasek Killer

Terrestrials

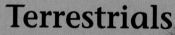

Black Ant   Dave's Cricket   Beetle   Whitlock Mouse   Osthoff Hopper

Nymphs

Gold Ribbed Hare's Ear   Pheasant Tail   Prince   Copper Bob   Soft-Hackle Woolly   Fast Sinking Scud   Chocolate Emerger

Streamers

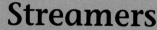

Mickey Finn   Muddler Minnow   Black Nose Dace   Bi-Bugger   Little Brown Trout

Specialty Flies

(Flies for trout and salmon, largemouth and smallmouth bass, walleye, northern pike and musky)

Bobbing Bait Fish

Bullet-Nose Diver

Red Woolly

Fly Pala

B.P. Musky

Bull-it-Head Frog

Tongue Depressor

Salmon Egg

Salmon Candy

Egg Sucking Stone

Double-Butt Glitter Bitch

JIM SCHOLLMEYER

Flies tied by Rich Osthoff, Bill Sherer, Bob White, Troy Wise, Orvis Company and the author.

Sources & Resources

Rustic Roads Board
Wisconsin Department of
Transportation
Rm 901
P.O. Box 7913
Madison, WI 53707-7913
608/266-0639

**State Historical Society of
Wisconsin**
816 State Street
Madison, WI 53706
608/264-6400

**Wisconsin Association of
Campground Owners (WACO)**
P.O. Box 580
Pardeeville, WI 53954
608/429-3061

Wisconsin B&B Association
108 South Cleveland Street
Merrill, WI 54452-2435
715/539-WBBA

Wisconsin Innkeepers Assoc.
509 W. Wisconsin Avenue,
Ste. 729
Milwaukee, WI 53203
414/271-2851

**Wisconsin Department of
Natural Resources**
Box 7921
Madison, WI 53707
608/266-2621

**Wisconsin Department of
Tourism**
201 W. Washington Avenue
Madison, WI 53707-7976
608/266-2161, 800/372-2737

**Wisconsin Department of
Transportation**
4802 Sheboygan Avenue
Madison, WI 53707
608/266-9434

**Apostle Islands National
Lakeshore**
Route 1, Box 4
Old Courthouse Building
Bayfield, WI 54814
715/779-3397

Chequamegon National Forest
1170 4th Avenue South
Park Falls, WI 54552
715/762-2461, 715/762-5701

Nicolet National Forest
68 South Stevens Street
Federal Building
Rhinelander, WI 54501
715/362-1300

St. Croix National Forest
P.O. Box 708
St. Croix Falls, WI 54024
715/483-3284

Adams County
Chamber of Commerce
P.O. Box 576
Adams, WI 53910-0576
608/339-6997, 888/339-6997

Algoma Area
Chamber of Commerce
1226 Lake Street
Algoma, WI 54201
920/487-2041, 800/498-4888

Antigo Area
Chamber of Commerce
P.O. Box 339
Antigo, WI 54409-0339
715/623-4134, 888/526-4523

Ashland Area
Chamber of Commerce
P.O. Box 746
Ashland, WI 54806-0746
715/682-2500, 800/284-9484

Baraboo Area
Chamber of Commerce
P.O. Box 442
Baraboo, WI 53913-0442
608/356-8333, 800/227-2266

Barron County
Clerk's Office
330 E. LaSalle Avenue
Barron, WI 54812-1588
715/537-6200

Bayfield
Chamber of Commerce
P.O. Box 138
Bayfield, WI 54814-0138
715/779-3335, 800/447-4094

Bayfield County
Tourism & Recreation
P.O. Box 832W
Washburn, WI 54891-0832
715/373-6125, 800/472-6338

Berlin
Chamber of Commerce
P.O. Box 128
Berlin, WI 54923-0128
920/361-3636, 800/979-9334

Black River Falls Area
Black River Area Chamber of
Commerce
336 N. Water Street
Black River Falls, WI 54615-1018
715/284-4658, 800/404-4008

Boscobel
Chamber of Commerce
P.O. Box 6
Boscobel, WI 53805-0006
608/375-2672

Boulder Junction
Chamber of Commerce
P.O. Box 286
Boulder Junction, WI 54512-0286
715/385-2400, 800/466-8759

Brown County
Parks Department
P.O. Box 23600
Green Bay, WI 54305-3600
920/448-4466

Buffalo County
Clerk's Office
P.O. Box 58
Alma, WI 54610-0058
608/685-6209

Burnett County
Department of Tourism &
Information
P.O. Box 49
Siren, WI 54872
715/349-7411, 800/788-3164

Burnett County
Resort/Campground Owners
Association
P.O. Box 48
Siren, WI 54872-0048
715/349-2000

Cable Area
Chamber of Commerce
P.O. Box 217
Cable, WI 54821-0217
715/798-3833, 800/533-7454

Chippewa Area
Visitors Center
10 S. Bridge Street
Chippewa Falls, WI 54729
715/723-0331, 888/723-0024

Chippewa Valley
Convention & Visitors Bureau
3625 Gateway Dr., Ste. F
Eau Claire, WI 54701
715/831-2345, 888/523-FUNN
(3866)

Clark County
Economic Development
Corporation
P.O. Box 236
Greenwood, WI 54437-0236
715/267-3205, 888/CLARK-WI,
888/252-7594

Clark County
Forestry & Parks Department
Courthouse
517 Court Street
Neillsville, WI 54456
715/743-5140, 888/CLARK-WI
(252-7594)

Columbia County
UWEX Office
P.O. Box 567
Portage, WI 53901-0567
608/742-9688

Crandon Area
Chamber of Commerce
P.O. Box 88
Crandon, WI 54520-0088
715/478-3450, 800/334-3387

Crawford County
UWEX Office
111 W. Dunn Street
Prairie du Chien, WI 53821
608/326-0224, 608/326-0223

Crivitz
Recreation Association
W13215 River Lane
Crivitz, WI 54114
715/757-2467, 800/CRIVITZ (

Dane County
(See Madison)

Dodge County
Tourism Association
127 E. Oak Street
Juneau, WI 53039
920/386-3705, 800/414-0101

Dodgeville
Chamber of Commerce Main
Street
178 1/2 N. Iowa Street, Ste. 210
Dodgeville, WI 53533-1546
608/935-9200, 608/935-5993

Door County
Chamber of Commerce
P.O. Box 406
Sturgeon Bay, WI 54235-0406
920/743-4456, 800/52-RELAX

Douglas County
(See Superior-Douglas County)

Dunn County
UWEX Office
390 Red Cedar Street, Ste. D
Menomonie, WI 54751-2265
715/232-1636

Eagle River Area
Chamber of Commerce & Visitors
Center
P.O. Box 1917
Eagle River, WI 54521-1917
715/479-6400, 800/359-6315

Eau Claire
(See Chippewa Valley)

Elroy Area
Advancement Corporation
P.O. Box 10
Elroy, WI 53929-0010
608/462-BIKE (2453), 888/606-
BIKE (2453)

Fennimore
Chamber and Economic
Development Office
P.O. Box 53
Fennimore, WI 53809-0053
608/822-3599, 800/822-1131

Fish Creek
Civic Association
P.O. Box 74
Fish Creek, WI 54212-0074
920/868-2316, 800/577-1880

Florence County
Natural Resource Center
HC1 Box 83
Florence, WI 54121
715/528-5377

Forest County
Advertising Committee
200 E. Madison
Crandon, WI 54520-1415
715/478-2212, 800/334-3387

Grant County
UWEX Office
P.O. Box 31
Lancaster, WI 53813-0031
608/723-2125

Grantsburg
Chamber of Commerce
P.O. Box 451
Grantsburg, WI 54840-0451
715/463-2405

Green Bay Area
Visitor & Convention Bureau
P.O. Box 10596
Green Bay, WI 54307-0596
920/494-9507, 888/867-3342

Green County
Tourism Committee Welcome
Center
2108 7th Avenue
Monroe, WI 53566
608/325-4636

Green Lake County
UWEX Office
P.O. Box 3188
Green Lake, WI 54941-3188
920/294-4032

Hayward Area
Chamber of Commerce
P.O. Box 726
Hayward, WI 54843-0726
715/634-8862, 800/724-2992

Hazelhurst
Information Center
P.O. Box 311
Hazelhurst, WI 54531-0311
715/356-7350

Hidden Valleys
P.O. Box 29
Richland Center, WI 53581-0029
608/647-2243

Hudson Area
Chamber of Commerce & Tourism
Bureau
502 Second Street
Hudson, WI 54016
715/386-8411, 800/657-6775

Iowa County
Clerk's Office
222 N. Iowa Street
Dodgeville, WI 53533
608/935-0399

Iron County
Development Zone Council
P.O. Box 97-WT
Hurley, WI 54534-0097
715/561-2922

Iron River Area
Chamber of Commerce
P.O. Box 448
Iron River, WI 54847-0448
715/372-8558

Kenosha Area
Convention & Visitors Bureau
812 56th Street
Kenosha, WI 53140-3734
414/654-7307, 800/654-7309

Kewaunee
Chamber of Commerce
P.O. Box 243
Kewaunee, WI 54216-0243
920/388-4822, 800/666-8214

Kewaunee County
Promotional Board
P.O. Box 211
Kewaunee, WI 54216-0211
920/388-4371

Kickapoo Valley
Association
P.O. Box 72
Soldiers Grove, WI 54655-0072
608/872-2504

Kickapoo Valley Reserve
505 North Mills
La Farge, WI 54639
608/625-2960

Kohler
Visitor Information Center
501 E. Highland Drive
Kohler, WI 53044
920/458-3450

La Crosse Area
Convention & Visitors Bureau
410 E. Veterans Memorial Drive
La Crosse, WI 54601-4990
608/782-2366, 877-LOVE-LAC
(568-3522)

Lafayette County
UWEX Office
627 Washington Street
Darlington, WI 53530-1396
608/776-4820

Langlade County
(See Antigo Area)

Lincoln County
Forestry, Land and Parks
1106 E. 8th Street
Merrill, WI 54452
715/536-0327

Madison
Greater Madison Convention &
Visitors Bureau
615 E. Washington Avenue
Madison, WI 53703-2952
608/255-2537, 800/373-6376

Manitowoc
Visitor & Convention Bureau
P.O. Box 966
Manitowoc, WI 54221-0966
920/683-4388, 800/627-4896 (US)

Manitowoc-Two Rivers Area
Chamber of Commerce
P.O. Box 903
Manitowoc, WI 54221-0903
920/684-5575, 800/262-7892

Marinette Area
Chamber of Commerce
P.O. Box 512
Marinette, WI 54143-0512
715/735-6681, 800/236-6681

Marinette County
UWEX Office
1926 Hall Avenue
Marinette, WI 54143-1717
715/732-7510

Marquette County
Clerk's Office
P.O. Box 186
Montello, WI 53949-0186
608/297-9114

Menominee
Tribal Public Relations
P.O. Box 910
Keshena, WI 54135-0910
715/799-5218, 715/799-5217

Menomonie
(See Chippewa Valley)

Merrill Area
Chamber of Commerce
720 E. Second Street
Merrill, WI 54452-1265
715-536-9474

Middleton
Chamber of Commerce
P.O. Box 620553
Middleton, WI 53562-0553
608/831-5696, 800/688-5694

Milwaukee
Greater Milwaukee Convention &
Visitors Bureau
510 W. Kilbourn Avenue
Milwaukee, WI 53203-1402
414/273-7222, 800/554-1448

Milwaukee County
Department of Parks, Recreation
& Culture
9480 Watertown Plank Road
Wauwatosa, WI 53226
414/257-6100

Monroe County
UWEX Office
P.O. Box 309
Sparta, WI 54656-0309
608/269-8722

Montello Area
Chamber of Commerce
P.O. Box 325
Montello, WI 53949-0325
608/297-7420, 800/684-7199

Mount Horeb Area
Chamber of Commerce
P.O. Box 84
Mount Horeb, WI 53572-0084
608/437-5914, 88-TROLLWAY
(888/765-5929)

New Glarus
Chamber of Commerce
P.O. Box 713
New Glarus, WI 53574-0713
608/527-2095, 800/527-6838

Oconto Area
Chamber of Commerce
P.O. Box 174
Oconto, WI 54153-0174
920/834-2255

Oconto County
Tourism
P.O. Box 43
Oconto, WI 54153-0043
920/834-6969, 888/626-6862

Oconto Falls Area
Chamber of Commerce
P.O. Box 24
Oconto Falls, WI 54154-0024
920/846-8306

Oneida County
Visitors Bureau
P.O. Box 795
Rhinelander, WI 54501-0795
715/365-7466, 800/236-3006

Osseo
City Hall
P.O. Box 308
Osseo, WI 54758-0308
715/597-2207

Ozaukee County
Tourism Council
P.O. Box 143
Port Washington, WI 53074-0143
414/377-9620, 800/403-9898

Pepin County
Economic Development
P.O. Box 39
Durand, WI 54736-0039
715/672-5709, 888/672-5709

Peshtigo
Chamber of Commerce
P.O. Box 36
Peshtigo, WI 54157-0036
715/582-0327

Phillips Area
Chamber of Commerce
305 S. Lake Street
Phillips, WI 54555-1352
715/339-4100

Pickerel-Pearson
Business Association
P.O. Box 76
Pickerel, WI 54465-0076
715/484-3901

Pierce County
Partners in Tourism, Inc.
P.O. Box 53
Ellsworth, WI 54011-0053
715/273-5864, 800/4-PIERCE

Polk County
Information Center
710 Hwy. 35 S
St. Croix Falls, WI 54024
715/483-1410, 800/222-POLK
(7655)

Port Washington
Tourism Council
P.O. Box 153
Port Washington, WI 53074-0153
414/284-0900, 800/719-4881

Portage Area
Chamber of Commerce
301 W. Wisconsin Street
Portage, WI 53901-2137
608/742-6242, 800/474-2525

Prairie du Chien
Chamber of Commerce
1305 Prairie Street
Prairie du Chien, WI 53821
608/326-8555, 800/PDC-1673
(U.S. & Canada)

Price County
Tourism Department
Price County Courthouse
126 Cherry Street
Phillips, WI 54555-1249
715/339-4505, 800/269-4505

Princeton Area
Greater Princeton Area Chamber
of Commerce
P.O. Box 45
Princeton, WI 54968-0045
920/295-3877, 920/295-3808

Racine County
Convention & Visitors Bureau
345 Main Street
Racine, WI 53403
414/634-3293, 800/272-2463

Rhinelander Area
Chamber of Commerce
P.O. Box 795
Rhinelander, WI 54501-0795
715/365-7464, 800/236-4386

Richland Area
Chamber/Main Street Partnership
P.O. Box 128
Richland Center, WI 53581-0128
608/647-6205, 800/422-1318

River Falls Area
Chamber of Commerce
409 Spruce Street
River Falls, WI 54022-2438
715/425-2533

Rock County
Tourism Council
P.O. Box 8041
Janesville, WI 53547-8041
800/48-PARKS, 800/423-5648

Rusk County
Visitor Center & Depot Museum
205 W. 9th Street S.
Ladysmith, WI 54848-2902

Sauk-Prairie Area
Chamber of Commerce
207 Water Street, Ste. D
Sauk City, WI 53583-1138
608/643-4168, 800/68-EAGLE

Sawyer County
Recreation Association
P.O. Box 351
Hayward, WI 54843-0351
715/462-3225, 800/72-HAYWARD

Shawano Area
Chamber of Commerce
P.O. Box 38
Shawano, WI 54166-0038
715/524-2139, 800/235-8528

Sheboygan County
Convention & Visitors Bureau
712 Riverfront Drive, #101
Sheboygan, WI 53081-4665
920/457-9495, 800/457-9497

Sheboygan Falls
Chamber/Main Street, Inc.
641 Monroe Street, Ste. 108
Sheboygan Falls, WI 53085-1337
920/467-6206

Sister Bay
Advancement Association
P.O. Box 351
Sister Bay, WI 54234-0351
920/854-2812

Southwest Wisconsin
Visitors Bureau
5754 Hwy. 23
Spring Green, WI 53588
608/935-3639, 800/947-2799

Sparta Area
Chamber of Commerce &
Tourism Promotion Bureau
111 Milwaukee Street
Sparta, WI 54656-2576
608/269-4123, 800/354-BIKE

Spring Green
Chamber of Commerce
P.O. Box 142
Spring Green, WI 53588-0142
608/588-2054, 608/588-2042,
800/588-2042

St. Croix County
Clerk's Office
1101 Carmichael Road
Hudson, WI 54016
715/386-4610

Stevens Point Area
Convention & Visitors Bureau
340 Division Street North
Stevens Point, WI 54481-1153
715/344-2556, 800/236-4636 (WI,
Chicago, Minneapolis)

Sturgeon Bay
Information Center
23 N. 5th Avenue
Sturgeon Bay, WI 54235-1713
920/743-3924

Superior-Douglas County
Convention & Visitors Bureau
305 E. Harborview Pkwy.
Superior, WI 54880
715/392-2773, 800/942-5313

Taylor County
Tourism Council
P.O. Box 172
Medford, WI 54451-0172
715/748-4729

Tomah
Chamber of Commerce and
Convention & Visitors Bureau
P.O. Box 625
Tomah, WI 54660-0625
608/372-2166, 800/94-TOMAH

Trempealeau County
Tourism Council
P.O. Box 21
Arcadia, WI 54612
608/323-7076, 800/927-5339

Two Rivers
Information Center
c/o Historical Society
1622 Jefferson Street
Two Rivers, WI 54241
920/793-2490

Uplands of Southwest Wisconsin
P.O. Box 202
Mount Horeb, WI 53572-0202
608/437-6580, 800/279-9472

Vernon County
Viroqua Chamber & Main Street
Program
220 S. Main Street
Viroqua, WI 54665-1650
608/637-2575

Verona Area
Chamber of Commerce
P.O. Box 930003
Verona, WI 53593-0003
608/845-5777

Vilas County
Advertising & Publicity
Department
330 Court Street
Eagle River, WI 54521
715/479-3649, 800/236-3649

Viroqua
(See Vernon County)

Walworth County
Tourism Council
P.O. Box 1015
Elkhorn, WI 53121-1015
414/723-3980, 800/395-8687

Washburn County
Tourism Association
122 N. River Street
Spooner, WI 54801-1445
715/635-9696, 800/367-3306

Washington County
Tourism Council
P.O. Box 122
West Bend, WI 53095-0122
414/335-4778, 414/255-2590

Waupaca Area
Chamber of Commerce
221 S. Main Street
Waupaca, WI 54981
715/258-7343, 888/417-4040

Wausau-Central Wisconsin
Convention & Visitors Bureau
10101 Market Street, Ste. C-80
Mosinee, WI 54455
715/355-8788, 888/WI-VISIT,
888/948-4748

Waushara County
Chamber of Commerce
P.O. Box 65
Wautoma, WI 54982-0065
920/787-7272

Westby
Tourist Information Center
200 N. Main Street
Westby, WI 54667-1305
608/634-4000

Westfield
Chamber of Commerce
P.O. Box 393
Westfield, WI 53964-0393
608/296-4146

Weyauwega
Area Chamber of Commerce
P.O. Box 531
Weyauwega, WI 54983-0531
920/867-2500

White Lake
Troutland Association
P.O. Box 245
White Lake, WI 54491-0245
715/882-8901

Wisconsin Dells
Visitor & Convention Bureau
P.O. Box 390
Wisconsin Dells, WI 54965-0390
608/254-4636, 800/22-DELLS

Wisconsin Dells-Lake Delton
Chamber of Commerce
P.O. Box 660
Wisconsin Dells, WI 53965-0660
608/253-5503, 800/94-DELLS

Wisconsin Indian Head Country
Tourism
P.O. Box 628
Chetek, WI 54728-0628
715/924-2970, 800/826-6966 (US),
800/472-6654 (WI)

Wood County
Park & Forestry Department
P.O. Box 8095
Wisconsin Rapids, WI 54495-8095
715/421-8422

Fly Shops (Bait & Tackle)

Angler's All
2803 E. Lakeshore Drive
Ashland, WI 54806
715/682-5754

Avalanche General Store
Rt. 30, Box 176B
Viroqua, WI 54665
608/634-2303

Bentley's Outfitters
582 Prairie Center Drive
Tower Square Shopping Center
Eden Prairie, MN 55344
612/828-9554

Bill Sherer's We Tie It
P.O. Box 516
10378 Main Street
Boulder Junction, WI 54512
715/385-0171

Bob Mitchell's Fly Shop
3394 Lake Elmo Avenue, N
Lake Elmo, MN 55042
651/770-5854

Bob's Bait & Tackle
1512 Velp Avenue
Green Bay, WI 54303
414/499-4737, 800/447-2312

Brule River Classics
6008 South State Road 27
Brule, WI 54820
715/372-8153

DIY Rod and Tackle
1304 Grange Avenue
Racine, WI 53405
414/633-8292

Eagle Sport Center
702 East Wall Street
Eagle River, WI 54521
715/479-8804

The Fly Angler
7500 University Avenue, N.E.
Minneapolis, MN 55432
612/572-0717

The Fly Fisher
8601 West Greenfield Avenue
West Allis, WI 53214
414/259-8100

Fly Rod And Tackle
1304 Grange Avenue
Racine, WI 53405
414/633-8292

Fontana Sports Specialties
251 State Street
Madison, WI 53703
608/257-5043

Gander Mountain
19555 W. Bluemound Road
Brookfield, WI 53045
414/785-4500

Gander Mountain
4045 Commonwealth
Eau Claire, WI 54701
715/833-7500

Gander Mountain
2002 Zeier Road
Madison, WI 53704
608/242-5700

Gander Mountain
9519 State Hwy. 16
Onalaska, WI 54650
608/783-2820

Gander Mountain
10201 Cty Trunk Hwy
Wausau, WI 54455
715/355-5500

Gander Mountain
12400 Fox River Road
Wilmot, WI 53192
414/862-2331

Laacke and Joys
1433 N. Water Street
Milwaukee, WI 53202
414/271-7878

Lunde's Fly Fishing Chalet
2491 Hwy. 92
Mt. Horeb, WI 53572
608/437-5465

Lund's Hardware
201 S. Main Street
River Falls, WI 54022
715/425-2415

Madison Outfitters
1335 S. Thompson Drive
Madison, WI 53716
608/833-1359

Mel's Trading Post
105 S. Brown Street
Rhinelander, WI 54501
715/362-5800

Mike's Mobile Service
Hwy. 64 & 55
Langlade, WI 54491
715/882-8901

Nickolai Sporting Goods
969 North Military Avenue
Green Bay, WI 54303
920/497-0275

The One Stop Sport Shop
1024 Main Street
Stevens Point, WI 54481
715/334-4540

Pastika's
P.O. Box 687
Hayward, WI 54843
715/634-4466

Rockin'K Fly Shop
E 5702 Spring Coulee Road
Coon Valley, WI 54623
608/452-3678

Scheel's All Sports
4800 Golf Road
Eau Claire, WI 54701
715/833-1886

Stark's Sport Shop
119 West Black Hawk Avenue
Prairie du Chien, WI 53821
608/326-2478

Steve Gerhardt Sporting Goods
3800 East Washington Avenue
Madison, WI 53704
608/244-2300

Sportsman's Choice
4033 US Hwy. 51 North
Janesville, WI 53545
608/752-6743

Spring Creek Angler
219 Central Avenue
Coon Valley, WI 54623
608/452-3430

Summit Fly Fishing Company
940 Grand Avenue
St. Paul, MN 55105
651/225-1200

The Superior Fly Angler
310 Belnap
Superior, WI 54880
715/395-54880

Wild Rose Fly Shop
430 Main Street
Wild Rose, WI 54984
920/622-4522

Wolf River Fly Shop
N4216 Rocky Rips Road
White Lake, WI 54491
715/882-5941

Fly Fishing Guides

Anglers All
2803 E. Lake Shore Drive
Ashland, WI 54806
715/682-5754

Rich Brown
2632 Greenwood
Wakegan,, WI 53703
847/263-0252

Flambeau Sports Outfitters
Steve Cervenka
N11151 Cty. Road F
Phillips, WI 54555
715/339-2012

Fontana Sports Specialties
251 State Street
Madison, WI 53703
608/257-5043

Chris Halla
1724 N. Whitney Drive
Appleton, WI 54914
920/731-2257

**Headwaters Fly Fishing
Company**
9667 103rd Place No.
Maple Grove, MN 55369
612/493-5800

Laacke & Joys
1433 N. Water Street
Milwaukee, WI 53202
414/271-7878

**Northern Adventures Guide
Service**
P.O. Box 516
Boulder Junction, WI 54512
715/385-0171

Rocking Trout
Clay Riness
P.O. Box 166
Coon Valley, WI 54623
608/452-3433

Bill Sherer
P.O. Box 516
Boulder Junction, WI 54512
715/385-0171

Spring Creek Angler
Dennis Graupe
219 Central Avenue
Coon Valley, WI 54623
608/452-3430

Manufacturers/
Suppliers

D.G. Schroeder Rod Company
3822 Brunswick Lane
Janesville, WI 53546
608/752-1520

LDH Landing Nets
530 West Redwing Street
Duluth, MN 55803
218/724-6283

Neil V. Sanvidge (nets)
White Lake, WI 54491

Rich Osthoff (flies)
N6868 Sandstone Drive
Mauston, WI 53948
608/847-5192

St. Croix Rod
P.O. Box 279
Park Falls, WI 54552
800/826-7042

Tomorrow River Rod, LLC
Dave Bell
8908 Highway GG
Almond, WI 54909
715/366-7105

We Tie It (flies)
Bill Sherer
P.O. Box 516
Boulder Junction, WI 54512
715/385-0171

Map Sources

**Northwoods Map Publishers,
Inc.**
P.O. Box 391
Boulder Junction, WI 54512

**Official State Highway Map of
Wisconsin**
Maps & Publications Sales
3617 Pierstorff Street
Madison, WI 53707-7713

Topo USA (software)
DeLorme
P.O. Box 298
Yarmouth, ME 04096
207/846-7000

Wisconsin Atlas & Gazetteer
DeLorme (see above listing)

**Wisconsin Department of
Tourism**
201 W. Washington Avenue
Madison, WI 53707-7976
800/372-2737

**Wisconsin Trout Fishing
Regulations and Guide**
Wisconsin Department of Natural
Resources
P.O. Box 7921
Madison, WI 53707-7921

**Wisconsin Trout Streams DNR
Publication 6-3600 (80)**
State Publications
222 North Midvale Boulevard
Suite 26
Madison, WI 53705
608/233-4710

Associations, Organizations,
Clubs

**Federation of Fly Fishers
(Contact national headquarters
for up-to-date information on
Wisconsin councils/chapters.)**
P.O. Box 1595
502 S. 19th Avenue
Bozeman, MT 59771
406/585-7592

River Alliance of Wisconsin
122 State Street
Suite 202
Madison, WI 53703
608/257-2424

Trout Unlimited (Contact national headquarters for up-to-date
information on Wisconsin councils/chapters)
1500 Wilson Boulevard
Suite 310
Arlington, VA 22209